QUINCY JONES

OVERCOMING ADVERSITY

QUINCY JONES

Linda Bayer, Ph.D.

Introduction by James Scott Brady,
Trustee, the Center to Prevent Handgun Violence
Vice Chairman, the Brain Injury Foundation

Chelsea House Publishers
Philadelphia

Dedication: The author would like to dedicate this book to Barbara Heiken and her parents, "Uncle Bob" and "Aunt Shirley" Rayburn. From the days when Barbara was my first readership for stories about the "Cape Codder Cat" to late-night talks with "Rabies" at summer camp, Barbara defined friendship fundamentally. Whether trying to finish a hundred maps or founding a company to fund nonprofit causes, Barbara brings humanity, humor, and compassion everywhere she goes in the world.

Frontis: A giant in the music world, Quincy Jones's artistry has influenced the course of American music for five decades. Nineteen ninety-six NAACP Image Awards Entertainer of the Year is only one of the scores of awards and honors he has earned as composer, arranger, director, and producer.

CHELSEA HOUSE PUBLISHERS

EDITORIAL DIRECTOR Stephen Reginald
PRODUCTION MANAGER Pamela Loos
ART DIRECTOR Sara Davis
DIRECTOR OF PHOTOGRAPHY Judy L. Hasday
MANAGING EDITOR James D. Gallagher
SENIOR PRODUCTION EDITOR J. Christopher Higgins

Staff for **Quincy Jones**
ASSOCIATE ART DIRECTOR Takeshi Takahashi
DESIGNER 21st Century Publishing and Communications, Inc.
COVER DESIGNER Keith Trego

COVER PHOTO Warner Bros. © by Warner Bros. Inc./Everett Collection, Inc.

© 2001 by Chelsea House Publishers, a subsidiary of Haights Cross Communications. All rights reserved. Printed and bound in the United States of America.
The Chelsea House World Wide Web address is
http://www.chelseahouse.com

First Printing

1 3 5 7 9 8 6 4 2

Library of Congress Cataloging-in-Publication Data

Bayer, Linda N.
Quincy Jones / by Linda Bayer.
    p.   cm. — (Overcoming adversity)
Includes bibliographical references and index.
Summary: A biography of the man who overcame childhood poverty and serious illness to become a successful composer, music arranger, and television producer.
ISBN 0-7910-5304-0 — ISBN 0-7910-5305-9 (pbk.)
1. Jones, Quincy, 1933–   —Juvenile literature. 2. Jazz musicians—United States —Biography—Juvenile literature. [1. Jones, Quincy, 1933–   . 2. Musicians. 3. Afro-Americans—Biography. 4. Jazz.] I. Title. II. Series.
ML3930.J63 B39 2000
781.64'092—dc21
[B]   00-020605
                                                                                      CIP

CONTENTS

OVERCOMING ADVERSITY

TIM ALLEN
comedian/performer

MAYA ANGELOU
author

APOLLO 13 MISSION
astronauts

LANCE ARMSTRONG
professional cyclist

DREW BARRYMORE
actress

JAMES BRADY
gun control activist

DREW CAREY
comedian/performer

JIM CARREY
comedian/performer

BILL CLINTON
U.S. president

TOM CRUISE
actor

MICHAEL J. FOX
actor

WHOOPI GOLDBERG
comedian/performer

EKATERINA GORDEEVA
figure skater

SCOTT HAMILTON
figure skater

JEWEL
singer and poet

JAMES EARL JONES
actor

QUINCY JONES
musician and producer

ABRAHAM LINCOLN
U.S. president

WILLIAM PENN
Pennsylvania's founder

JACKIE ROBINSON
baseball legend

ROSEANNE
entertainer

MONICA SELES
tennis star

SAMMY SOSA
baseball star

DAVE THOMAS
entrepreneur

SHANIA TWAIN
entertainer

ROBIN WILLIAMS
performer

STEVIE WONDER
entertainer

ON FACING ADVERSITY

James Scott Brady

I GUESS IT'S a long way from a Centralia, Illinois, train yard to the George Washington University Hospital Trauma Unit. My dad was a yardmaster for the old Chicago, Burlington & Quincy Railroad. As a child, I used to get to sit in the engineer's lap and imagine what it was like to drive that train. I guess I always have liked being in the "driver's seat."

Years later, however, my interest turned from driving trains to driving campaigns. In 1979, former Texas governor John Connally hired me as a press secretary in his campaign for the American presidency. We lost the Republican primary to a former Hollywood star named Ronald Reagan. But I managed to jump over to the Reagan campaign. When Reagan was elected in 1980, I was "sitting in the catbird seat," as humorist James Thurber would say—poised to be named presidential press secretary. I held that title throughout the eight years of the Reagan administration. But not without one terrible, extended interruption.

It happened barely two months after the Reagan administration took office. I never even heard the shots. On March 30, 1981, my life went blank in an instant. In an attempt to assassinate President Reagan, John Hinckley Jr. armed himself with a "Saturday night special"—a low-quality, $29 pistol—and shot wildly as our presidential entourage exited a Washington hotel. One of the exploding bullets struck me just above the left eye. It shattered into a couple dozen fragments, some of which penetrated my skull and entered my brain.

The next few months of my life were a nightmare of repeated surgery, broken contact with the outside world, and a variety of medical complications. More than once, I was very close to death.

The next few years were filled with frustrating struggles to function with a paralyzed right side, struggles to speak and communicate.

To people who face and defeat daunting obstacles, "ambition" is not becoming wealthy or famous or winning elections or awards. Words like "ambition" and "achievement" and "success" take on very different meanings. The objective is just to live, to wake up every morning. The goals are not lofty; they are very ordinary.

My own heroes are ordinary folks—but they accomplish extraordinary things because they try. My greatest hero is my wife, Sarah. She's accomplished a lot of things in life, but two stand out. The first has been the way she has cared for me and our son since I was shot. A tremendous tragedy and burden was dropped unexpectedly into her life, totally beyond her control and without justification. She could have given up; instead, she focused her energies on preserving our family and returning our lives to normal as much as possible. Week by week, month by month, year by year, she has not reached for the miraculous, just for the normal. Yet in focusing on the normal, she has helped accomplish the miraculous.

Her other most remarkable accomplishment, to me, has been spearheading the effort to keep guns out of the hands of criminals and children in America. Opponents call her a "gun grabber"; I call her a national hero. And I am not alone.

After a seven-year battle, during which Sarah and I worked tirelessly to educate the public about the need for stronger gun laws, the Brady Bill became law in 1993. It was a victory, achieved in the face of tremendous opposition, that now benefits all Americans. From the time the law took effect through fall 1997, background checks had stopped 173,000 criminals and other high-risk purchasers from buying handguns, and the law has helped to reduce illegal gun trafficking.

Sarah was not pursuing fame, or even recognition. She simply started at one point—when our son, Scott, found a loaded handgun on the seat of a pickup truck and, thinking it was a toy, pointed it at Sarah.

Fortunately, no one was hurt. But seeing a gun nearly bring a second tragedy upon our family, Sarah became determined to do whatever she could to prevent senseless death and injury from guns.

Some people think of Sarah as a powerful political force. To me, she's the person who so many times fed me and helped me dress during my long years of recovery.

Overcoming obstacles is part of life, not just for people who are challenged by disabilities, illnesses, or tragedies, but for all people. No matter what the obstacle—fear, disability, prejudice, grief, or a difficulty that isn't likely to "just go away"—we can all work to make this world a better place.

Quincy Jones's musical gifts have brought him fame and fortune, but with all his honors and accolades, he remembers his roots in Chicago's ghetto, reminding others, "I never forget where I came from."

1

LUCKY TO BE ALIVE

CHICAGO—THE "CITY OF BIG SHOULDERS," as poet Carl Sandburg memorialized it—offers the promise of better things to those who work hard. But in the early 1930s, at the height of the Great Depression, more families were shivering in the wind off Lake Michigan than could be protected by even the strongest town.

In a poor neighborhood on the South Side of Chicago, two recent newcomers to the "Windy City" were rejoicing in the birth of a son on March 14, 1933. They named the child after his father: Quincy Delight Jones Jr. As they held their squalling infant, Quincy Sr. and Sarah Wells Jones had no way of knowing that their son would one day be a powerful and influential figure in the entertainment industry.

Both of Quincy Jr.'s parents had left racism and segregation in the South, hoping to make a new start in the industrial North. In the decades after the Civil War, northern cities like New York, Detroit, Philadelphia, Cleveland, and Chicago offered African Americans a measure of freedom from prejudice and hatred that they could not find in the South.

The descendants of former slaves migrated north, searching for the American Dream.

Unfortunately, at the time Quincy Jr. was born many of the factories were closed or operated with skeleton crews because of the depression. It was difficult for many people, especially African Americans, to find work. Quincy Jones Sr. looked for work as a carpenter. Jobs were hard to find, and many a family was torn apart by economic hardship and emotional despair.

In the case of the Jones household, the mother's state of mind made matters worse. Sarah began to suffer from chronic mental illness shortly after Quincy's birth, and for most of the boy's life his mother was in and out of mental institutions. Quincy still remembers one birthday party that was ruined when his mother smashed the cake in the backyard. "There's no question that she pushed me into a fantasy world. I used to sit for hours in the closet and just dream," Quincy told a reporter from *People* magazine in 1990.

When Sarah Jones became ill, she was taken to a mental hospital. Quincy and his brother were bewildered by their mother's disappearance. He was too young to understand; instead, Quincy blamed his mother for her absence. He often thought, "Well, I can't depend on my mother because I don't have one." For most of his life, he felt anger and grief in connection with her. He didn't think about the possibility his musical gift might have come from his mother, a very religious woman who knew how to play the piano and loved music. (Sarah Jones would one day help found the Seattle Religious Art Society, which sponsored concerts and educational opportunities for young people.)

Many years later, he was able to be more objective. "At one point, I stopped thinking about myself, and I started to think about my mother and how much she loved us. And I got it, you know? It was real late, but . . ." Quincy went on to discuss the difficulty of trying "to convert hate into love. And that's a tough trick. But if you do it, it's the only salvation."

But it was music, Sarah Jones's first love, that would one day make her son rich and famous. On his grandmother's old Victrola record player, Quincy heard the sounds of such jazz greats as Fats Waller and Duke Ellington. Proximity to a musically inclined neighbor also helped. "When I was five or six, back in Chicago, there was this lady named Lucy Jackson who used to play stride piano in the apartment next door, and I listened to her all the time right through the wall," Quincy later told author Alex Haley.

By the time Quincy Jones was in his 40s, he had composed or arranged music for nearly every great singer or musician in the contemporary entertainment industry— Frank Sinatra, Count Basie, trumpeter Dizzy Gillespie, and pop superstar Michael Jackson among them. He collaborated on the music for movies and television shows, and even produced hit TV programs. With scores of pictures to his credit, Quincy won Grammy Awards for his music year after year. Yet he never lost his sense of humility. "I never forget where I came from, man," he later told interviewers:

> When I was seven, I remember my brother Lloyd and I went to spend the summer with my grandmother in Louisville, Kentucky. She was an ex-slave, but she'd moved up in the world since then. The lock on the back door of her little house was a nail, and she had a coal stove and kerosene lamps for light, and she used to tell us to go down to the river in the evening and catch us a rat, and we'd take that sucker home in a bag and she'd cook it up for supper. She fried it with onions, and it tasted *good*, man. When you're seven years old and you don't know any better, everything tastes good to you. That kind of memory makes you appreciate everything that much more because from then on, no matter how good it gets, you never take anything for granted. I've had the whole range of experiences, from rats to *paté*, and I feel lucky just to be alive.

Quincy Jones doesn't just "feel" lucky to be alive: he *is*. In 1974 a near-fatal aneurysm—or hemorrhaging in the

In the course of his career, Quincy has collaborated with most of the entertainers in the music industry, composing and arranging music for greats from Count Basie to Michael Jackson. He also has countless films and television shows to his credit, including the 1996 Academy Awards telecast, which he produced, and on which he appears here with Arthur Hiller, president of the Academy of Motion Picture Arts and Sciences, to announce best actor nominations.

head—almost killed Quincy and required two dangerous brain surgeries to save his life. In addition to this life-threatening illness, overwork and absorption in his career led to multiple divorces and broken homes for the five children (four daughters and a son) Quincy sired with a series of wives and companions. Quincy regrets his absence from the lives of his children during their early years. He also recognizes that a nervous breakdown he suffered at midlife was in part a crisis of conscience because he had neglected to find values—outside of a love for music—that were worthy of devotion.

Quincy Jones's odyssey—his rise to fame and fortune, confrontation with racism, and travels throughout the world—reflects the evolution of the American Dream over the past six decades, when legal discrimination against blacks, women, and other minorities began to give way to a more equal society. The development of Quincy Jones's artistic style exemplifies the profound changes in U.S. music from folk, country, gospel, show tunes, and big band to blues, rock, soul, jazz, heavy metal, and rap. Quincy adopted electronic instruments and participated in a technological revolution that shook the recording industry, which in turn influenced music in the United States and around the world. Quincy Jones's success in business—both in New York and Hollywood—is an American tale that illustrates the many-sided nature of his talent.

Chicago's teeming ghetto during the Great Depression of the 1930s was Quincy's early childhood home. When his father moved the family west to the state of Washington, young Quincy found the opportunity to develop his musical talents and take the first steps that would lead to his career as musician and performer.

2

FROM ADOLESCENCE TO EARLY ADULTHOOD

QUINCY GREW UP on the South Side of Chicago, which he termed "the biggest ghetto in the world." Every street was a territory ruled by a gang, and the preferred weapon of survival was a switchblade. To these gangs, the issue of race was a main ingredient in their constant rebellion against society.

Quincy's brother Lloyd later spoke about an incident that typified the violence they encountered. "On the way to school one day when we were six or seven, we stopped and saw this guy hanging by the back of his coat on the first rung of a telephone pole, with an ice pick stuck through his neck," he recalled. "We checked that out and went right on to school."

Quincy remembered seeing "Two Gun Pete," a famous Chicago cop, shooting a gang member at a local drug store. "My mind was not mature enough really to feel sympathy. . . . I just accepted it as part of Chicago life. And I accepted color hatred as another part of it."

In a sociological study titled *Black Metropolis,* Richard Wright—who, like Quincy's mother, also came to Chicago in the 1930s from Mississippi—wrote about the Chicago that shaped Quincy's early days: "That great iron city, that impersonal, mechanical city, amid the steam, the smoke, the snowy winds, the blistering suns. . . . Many migrants like us were driven and pursued, in the manner of characters in a Greek play, down the paths of defeat; but luck must have been with us, for we somehow survived."

When Quincy was not in school, his part-time job as an errand boy for a local laundry helped keep him out of trouble. "My first taste of responsibility" is the way Quincy described the job he held when he was seven. He had to be responsible; his parents divorced around this time.

Quincy's neighborhood did have one celebrity resident, a boxer named Joe Louis who was the heavyweight champion of the world. Louis (nicknamed the Brown Bomber) was an acquaintance of Quincy Sr. When the elder Jones took his sons to see a Joe Louis fight, though, he had no way of knowing the violence of the ring would eventually lead him to love. "Daddy had taken Lloyd and me to one of Joe Louis's fights, and Joe Louis gave us the boxing gloves that he won with," Quincy Jr. later recalled. "Waymond, who lived down the street, had a BB gun, and I really wanted it bad. So I said, 'I'll trade you these boxing gloves for this BB gun!' Well, I went home, and my daddy was mad. He went back to retrieve the gloves, and when he came back he was in love with Waymond's mother, Elvira."

Quincy was 10 years old when his father remarried. On July 4, 1943, the new family—which included Quincy's stepmother Elvira and her three children—moved west to Bremerton, Washington, in hopes of starting over again. As was often the case, Quincy didn't receive much preparation for this change in his life. He and his brother were getting haircuts in the afternoon when their father arrived with the luggage packed and Trailways bus tickets in

hand. (No doubt Quincy's birth mother, who was in a mental institution, wasn't given much warning, either. After her release Sarah Jones also moved to the Seattle area, where she became involved in church and education programs.)

Near Seattle, Mr. Jones landed a job as a carpenter at the naval shipyards, and the family was able to move into a decent neighborhood. At school, Quincy was "the only black kid in the class—and the other kids were wonderful to me. Positively no problems. Completely integrated." This contrast to Chicago, where even the gangs were

Boxing great Joe Louis (right) lands a blow on German challenger Max Schmeling in 1936. Louis won the world heavyweight championship in 1937 and held the belt for 12 years. Thousands of African Americans like Quincy looked to Joe Louis with pride as a symbol of black achievement.

racially segregated, was quite a surprise for Quincy.

> It took me a few months before I realized I didn't have to carry my switchblade anymore. The school I went to was like a model of multi-racial integration, and the kids got along together about as well as they do anywhere in the world. But it's not like we moved to Disneyland. There's no way you're going to live anywhere in America and not feel the pangs of racial prejudice. You still got the *hate* stare from certain kinds of white people, but that's a daily experience from the time you're two years old, and you learn to deal with it.

In retrospect, Quincy said, "The greatest contribution that my dad made was getting us out of Chicago." The house where the new "blended" family went to live had just one bedroom, a living space, and a kitchen. Ten people were living in two rooms, and the number of residents was growing. In addition to Quincy Sr. and Elvira, under one roof lived Quincy and Lloyd, "Katherine, who's my stepsister; Waymond who's my half-brother; and Margie who's my half-sister; and later there was Janet, my half-sister; and Richard, my half-brother; and Willie Lee, Theresa. . . . I can't keep up with my Daddy," Quincy remarked.

Not surprisingly, there was friction in such close quarters. "As far as the kids were concerned, we all got along. It was the parent-child situation that didn't seem to work," said Quincy. A closet in the Jones home was an island of sanctuary amid strife. Years later, Quincy told Henry Louis Gates of Harvard University, "I used to go into this little closet" and block out "everything negative that happened to me. I would try to find a way to go into this other world, a music world, and just get out of whatever . . . I couldn't handle. I've been crawling into that world for a long time. Beauty and creativity convert that same energy—you can use it. What comes out bitterness destroys you, and I'm not going to destroy myself so it's a conversion. It's like taking garbage and making recycled paper out of it."

The rectangular wooden house, with two windows and a door on the long side, actually had a white picket fence out front and a white-framed screen door above three wooden steps, but house number 4926—as the sign under the front lamp read—was virtually indistinguishable from the shack next door. "We lived in a place way out of town, way up on a hill called Sinclair Heights. It was the black section of the city. If you were a brother, that's where you lived. You had to walk three miles up that hill. It was like a ghetto project, but it was all new and it looked so good," Quincy remembers.

As an enterprising adolescent among so many children, Quincy Jones was willing to work hard at almost anything to earn money. His jobs ranged from shining shoes and babysitting to picking strawberries, delivering newspapers, washing windows, working for a dry cleaner, and setting pins in a bowling alley. Quincy also ran errands for pimps and prostitutes.

A barbershop in Seattle was the site of a major change in Quincy's life. When not busy at one odd job or another, the future musician used to hang out at the Sinclair Heights Barbershop where Eddie Lewis, the proprietor, played the trumpet. Quincy was captivated by this instrument, and playing it soon replaced his other extracurricular activities. Quincy joined the school choir and band. In addition to the trumpet, he learned to play the snare and bass drums, timpani, tuba, B-flat baritone horn, French horn, E-flat alto sax, sousaphone, and piano. "I really wanted to learn trombone so I could march right behind the drum majorettes. Then my father gave me a trumpet of my own, and soon I was wearing one of those red-and-white derbies and doo-wopping with my plunger mute in the National Guard band."

In 1947 14-year-old Quincy made his professional debut, earning seven dollars for an appearance with a band

Playing with Blackwell's band in Seattle, Quincy performed with many well-known visiting African-American entertainers, among them Billie Holiday. Nicknamed "Lady Day," she sang with major bands and in clubs across the country, and was considered one of the most important jazz singers of her time.

at the Bremerton YMCA. Music soon became more than a pastime for Quincy, who was drawn to the traveling African-American entertainers who played in the port city. When he wasn't playing in band concerts or singing in a gospel group, Quincy would be performing in places like the Seattle Tennis Club. Wearing a white tuxedo, he played songs like "Room Full of Roses" for all-white audiences. Afterward, Quincy would make the rounds of the all-black "get-down clubs" like the Reverend Silas Groves's Washington Social and Education Club—"which was nothing but a juke joint with strippers," he later commented—or the Black and Tan, where he played R&B (rhythm-and-blues) for Bumps Blackwell, a local bandleader and music promoter who eventually "discovered" Sam Cooke and Little Richard.

Bumps had many different jobs in Bremerton: he

worked at a butcher shop and a jewelry store, drove a taxi-cab, and performed with various bands. Jones and the other members of Blackwell's band were proud to be the ones who played when Billie Holiday came to town. But Quincy's act involved more than just playing the horn. "We danced, we sang, we did everything. We had two girl singers . . . four horns, a rhythm section, a male singer, and two comedians—that was me and a friend of mine. We doubled as the comedy team." At 2 A.M., Quincy would end up at the Elks Club, playing bebop until dawn for himself and the other musicians.

In the introduction to *Q's Jook Joint*, a book of Quincy's scores published to mark his 50th year in music, Jones presented some historical information on this type of hangout. "The European-American word 'joint' has been known since the latter part of the nineteenth century, indicating an unpretentious commercial establishment, principally for eating and drinking, and often providing music for dancing. The word 'jook' [also spelled 'juke'] basically means to have fun dancing and socializing in clubs and similar places."

He added that, "'jook' derives from West African languages, for example, in the Wolof *dzug*, or the Bambara *dzugu*, where it means 'wicked' or 'unsavory.' The expression 'jook joint,' then, must have been coined in the African-American community sometime before 1900 to describe a simple place where you could go to have a good time. The fact that it is named for 'wickedness' indicates that, for some people, it spelled trouble."

The significance of the jook joint in urban black culture cannot be underestimated. From 1900 to the middle of the century, nearly 75 percent of African Americans migrated from poor rural areas to the cities. In Chicago alone, the black population grew tenfold in 40 years. As with all migrants, aspects of their previous culture were brought over and adapted to their new environment. The earthy, energetic music of the jook joints—now known as dance halls, speakeasies, or blues bars—can be seen as the precursor to the revolutionary rock 'n' roll of the 1950s.

Music functioned in Quincy Jones's life like the closet in his house where he hid from sorrow. "To get out of whatever was distasteful or unpleasant or uncomfortable or painful, music could always soothe. You just crawl in that world and reach in that black hole and grab something beautiful, and it would take you away from all of that." Quincy understood many art forms in this way. Creative endeavors of all sorts helped tortured people escape from despair. Quincy Jones interpreted comedy from this perspective.

In a foreword he wrote years later to a book called *Snaps*, Quincy explained that "playing the dozens" was a word game, a style of joking, that referred to the "dirty dozen" (the worst twelve slaves who were sold together at a bargain rate after getting off a ship). Making degrading remarks about the dozen—much like telling jokes about "your mama"—was a way of saying the opposite of what was meant since a person's mother was among the most beloved individuals to a child whose family, as well as his race, was not respected by the larger culture. Saying the reverse of the truth, in jest, was a way to approach the unspeakable reality in a society that routinely lied about black people. "Like music, the dozens has lyrics, cadence, and rhythm. The words might seem rough, but you can't take them literally. Similar to the blues, the dozens is a conversion of pain into joy. This battle of words is a song of survival. Slaves practiced the 'game' to offset the pain of not being able to express their true feelings in front of their masters," wrote Quincy Jones. He concluded the introduction with a statement that might also apply to his music: "The dozens is a style of humor that enables us to deal with the pain in our lives. It's a serious art and tradition. It's part of our folklore."

In an interview, Quincy once said, "If just one person believes in you, then the responsibility isn't only to yourself.

It's to another person." Quincy learned this lesson in school from a friend. A white boy named Robin Fields once encouraged him to run for boys' club president, with Fields as his manager. Quincy thought the idea was ridiculous, since only 30 of the 2,800 students were black. Nonetheless, Fields persisted and Quincy won the election.

When Quincy was about 14, he was arrested with a group of others who were smoking marijuana. "Boy, that process was not fun," he later recalled. "The cops stopped us. They saw five black dudes in the car, and they pulled us over. They smelled the stuff, and we were the headlines on the *Bremerton Sun* the next day."

Quincy has since mourned the loss of people "who went into a cocoon" with alcohol, drugs, or other forms of destructive behavior when the world had no place for their talents. Quincy speaks of substance abuse as

> an epidemic that has the potential to bring *civilization* to its knees and, frankly, I don't know how we're going to make it through 'cause we're going to lose a whole generation of kids to drugs and drug dealing. How are you gonna save them when they're dangling $1800 a day in front of thirteen-year-olds to sell dope? You can't tempt them with the promise of a college degree when they see brothers with masters degrees carrying bags at the airport or pushing fries at the Burger King. . . . We'd better do something about it before it's too late.

Luckily, Quincy Jones himself didn't fall victim to booze or dope like so many musicians from his generation that the entertainment industry lost to deadly intoxicants. Quincy clung to his dream, which lead him out of the streets toward fortune and fame.

Within Quincy's own family, there was some interest in music. Quincy's father helped organize a small choir at a local church. He was raised Catholic, yet he was drawn to the Baptist and Sanctified churches because the music projected more personal feelings.

Bandleader, singer, and dancer Cab Calloway was a sensation in the clubs and led one of the most successful bands of the swing-music era. He later recorded music for famous entertainers as well as for films, opera (Porgy and Bess)*, and Broadway.*

Although Quincy's father was no musician, he supported his son's budding ambition. Quincy explained, "My daddy did the best he could, you know? He always encouraged whatever I was into. There were so many kids, and I wanted a music book in Bremerton, and it cost ninety-eight cents or something, and he would sneak the money to me because he didn't have enough to give to everybody. He was beautiful."

Quincy started singing spirituals under Joseph Powe, "who at one time had been with Wings over Jordan. He was at the same time leader of a U.S. Navy dance band, and he taught me a lot about pulsation and phrasing.

"After singing with him, I started on piano," Quincy continued. "Then I was student-manager for the Robert E. Coontz High School band. . . . From then on, I was in every

Count Basie, a pianist and big-band leader, was an early mentor and role model for young Quincy Jones. Basie's orchestra performed with some of the best singers and instrumentalists of the time.

musical organization in school until I graduated—chorus, orchestra, dance band, etc."

Quincy's interest in jazz started during these years. "It began when Cab Calloway came to play in Seattle, and I was part of a local band that played opposite him." Quincy remembers: "After Cab left, Billie Holiday came and the band I was with had to accompany her. Bobby Tucker was Lady's pianist then. I've loved him ever since. He was so patient when he rehearsed us. We didn't read music too fast at that time."

Another musician who was a great influence on young Quincy Jones was big-band leader Count Basie. Quincy was 13 when the bandleader visited Seattle with his septet (a seven-piece band). "At that time, he was the biggest and the best big-band leader in the world, but he

Quincy's interest in jazz was sparked by bands like this one that played in the "Golden Age" of jazz music. Listening to bands, going to concerts, and hanging out with visiting musicians encouraged the young player to compose and orchestrate his own music.

took me under his wing, and we formed a relationship that lasted the rest of his life," Quincy later said. "He was my uncle, my father, my mentor, my friend." Basie's trumpet man, Clark Terry, showed Quincy how to improve his act. "Clark showed me how wrong I was playing and that I had a very bad lip position. I was playing under the lip. And he showed me how to get around these problems." He gave Quincy the confidence to get out there and see what he could do. "They were my idols as musicians, but even more important, they were my role models as human beings."

Another influence was Ray Charles, the legendary blind musician, who was only two years older than Quincy Jones. "When I was about fourteen, I went over to Bumps' house one night, and there he was—this sixteen-year-old blind kid playing the piano and singing 'Blowing the Blues Away.' He was so good he gave me goose bumps," Quincy later recalled. "He already had his own apartment, he had all these women, he owned four or five suits. He was doing better than me, and he was *blind*, man. So, I just attached myself to him, and he became like a big brother to me. Taught me how to read and write music in braille and how to voice horns and how to deal with polytonality, and that opened up a golden door for me." Now Quincy was able to explore how all the different instruments he had learned to play could be woven together into the fabric of a song. He became fascinated with orchestration and arranging.

In the beginning, Quincy used to go to concerts and study the musicians. During intermission and after the show, he would go up on the stage and ask questions. He'd concentrate on the musical score, and the musicians were often so impressed with his interest they helped him as much as they could. Later, Quincy would carry an instrument with him backstage before or after a performance, knowing that with a trumpet or trombone in hand he'd blend in with the musicians and not get stopped. He admits to being influenced by "Lester Young, Dizzy Gillespie and, of course, Charlie Parker," as well as by vibraphonist Lionel Hampton. "I kept hanging out with whoever was in town, until finally when I was fifteen [Lionel Hampton] gave me the chance to blow trumpet and write some arrangements for the band," Quincy later recalled. "Well, that's all the encouragement I needed to pack up and get on the bus. Only before we could pull out, his wife Gladys caught me on board and yanked me back onto the street. 'That boy's gonna finish his schooling before he gets back on this bus,' she told Hamp. So, I was highly motivated to finish school so I could go join the band."

In 1947, Quincy's family moved from Bremerton to Seattle. In 1948 Quincy wrote a suite (a long musical composition that has several movements of different character) called "From the Four Winds." This first composition "was quite long, more than twenty minutes, and eventually it got me a scholarship to Seattle University." Quincy was awarded that honor in 1950—the same year his composition "Nocturne in Blue" was performed at a high school recital. Unfortunately, Quincy found the modern music department "disappointing" at Seattle University.

After graduating from high school, Quincy completed one semester at Seattle University. The following year, Quincy was offered a scholarship to Schillinger House of Music (now called Berklee School of Music) in Boston. "Boston was the farthest I'd ever been from home, and it was close to New York," said Quincy. He studied at Berklee for nearly a year—sometimes taking up to 10 classes a day—and supplemented his scholarship by working semiprofessionally with bands at a number of strip joints.

Quincy got his first taste of the "Big Apple" in 1951 when he took a train from Boston to New York, where he had been hired to arrange some music for a recording session with Oscar Pettiford, a friend from Seattle. Quincy was paid $17 a song, but more important was the opportunity to interact with other talented musicians.

After the session was done, Quincy and Pettiford hit the nightclubs on 52nd street, including Birdland, a world-famous Broadway nightclub named after Charlie "Bird" Parker. Owned by music mogul and reputed mobster Morris Levy, the basement club was a magnet for promising young musicians and "hipsters" who liked "bebop"—a style of music in which the skill of a soloist is highlighted as players improvise and compete with one another, stretching the melodic and rhythmic line.

When Quincy actually met Charlie Parker, he was terribly excited—until the musician burst the boy's bubble of joy. "We went to Big Nick's on 110th," Quincy remembers, "and Bird said: 'Let's buy some weed.' And

Quincy celebrates his 1996 Entertainer of the Year Award with an affectionate hug for longtime friend Ray Charles. For young Quincy, the legendary singer and pianist, who encouraged and guided him toward a music career, was an inspiring example of what black musicians could achieve.

I said, 'that's hip.' When you're eighteen years old, you want to be down with the dudes."

Quincy had about twenty dollars left from the two arrangements, and Parker offered to hold the money for him. "It started raining, and we were out in front of this raggedy place on 139th. Bird said, 'You stay right here. We'll be right back.' After forty minutes, I was starting to get the message. Then I started to cry." Parker had stolen money from his teenaged admirer, who in turn had to walk all the way back to midtown. Quincy learned something that night about drugs and what they do to people who take them. In fact, Charlie Parker died within four years of that humiliating evening. A benefit was held at Carnegie Hall, and $13,000 was raised to help support Parker's children. "It's too bad they didn't give that kind of money to him when he was alive," Quincy wrote to Raymond Horricks. "Financial insecurity was one of the chief causes of his death."

Quincy often traveled from Boston to New York on weekends. Quincy was introduced to Art Tatum, pianist Thelonious Monk, and Miles Davis. "It was like a fairy story," Quincy remembers. The local musicians in Boston also taught Quincy what they could. For a few weeks, Quincy had gone on the road with Jay "Hootie" McShann. "It was a very uncertain band with Jay not always showing up at rehearsals," Quincy recalls. Looking back at this period, Quincy concluded, "with McShann I gained invaluable experience in writing and playing, but most of all I discovered the financial insecurity of the music business."

Quincy was still anxious to play with Lionel Hampton's band, in keeping with the promise made when he was in high school. "Hamp" suddenly made good on the old offer: "Okay, you're of age now. You can join the band," said Lionel. Quincy was delighted. "I left school and said I'd be back in a couple of months—I lied," Quincy recalls. However, Quincy says that at the time he did think he'd be back in school sooner. In any case, the young musician correctly perceived that "the best kind of schooling in the world is to put the academic thing together with what's really out there. I got to meet an incredible group of musicians with Hampton. So I stayed nearly three years, and we went to Europe in 1953—which really opened my head up."

With Hampton, Quincy first went to New York and then on tour throughout the South. Lionel Hampton's outfit featured strong rhythms, a honking tenor sax, and a screaming trumpet. "Hamp" played the vibraphone and was quite a showman in a purple coat with matching shorts, socks,

Lionel Hampton's flamboyant style as bandleader did not impress young Quincy. Joining the band and touring, however, was Quincy's big break, giving him the opportunity to play and learn from several talented musicians, whom he admired and wanted to emulate.

shoes, and Tyrolean hats. Quincy was mortified by the bandleader's outfits, but ecstatic to be in the band. "I was eighteen, and it was like going to heaven for me," Quincy remembers. "That's where all my idols were: Oscar Pettiford was like my big brother, and he introduced me to all of them: Miles, Dizzy, Ray Brown, Charlie Parker, Thelonious Monk, Charlie Mingus, all the beebop dudes. They were the new generation of jazz musicians."

Quincy got a dose of reality when he toured the American South with Hampton's band in the 1950s. Unused to segregation in the North, he was stunned and angry at the discrimination and decided that only in Europe could he be recognized for his talent, not his color.

3

LEAVING HOME TO CHASE THE STARS

TRAVELING THROUGH THE South with a band was an education for Quincy, and music was not the only subject. A crash course in "Racism 101" introduced Quincy to a side of America he'd never seen before. Between 1951 and 1959, Quincy played off and on with Lionel Hampton, visiting every state in America. After they left New York, Hamp's band went on a long tour through the South, including 79 one-nighters in a row in the Carolinas alone. "Every night was like going into a battle zone," Quincy recalled. "About two-thirds of the way through the show, somebody out on the dance floor would start a fight, and before the evening was over there'd be two or three stabbings. You got used to that kind of thing."

What Quincy didn't get used to was the discrimination. It was on that trip that he got his first real exposure to segregation. For an African American, visiting the South was like being in enemy territory. He relied on the older musicians, those who had been on the road for years, and they had seen it all. Once in Texas, they pulled into a little town around five in the morning, and an effigy of a black person with a rope around his neck was hanging from the steeple of the biggest church in town.

The other band members told him, "Don't feel so bad. It's no different for Lena Horne or Sammy Davis Jr. or Harry Belafonte. They may be big stars, but when they play Vegas, they still got to eat in the kitchen, they can't stay in the hotel where they're working, they can't even mingle out front with the people who just paid to see them on the stage." Quincy realized if he wanted to be treated like a person and appreciated for his musical talent, Europe was the place to go.

Before leaving for Europe in 1953, however, Quincy married his high school sweetheart. He had met Jeri Caldwell when he was 15 years old, and she moved to New York with Quincy when he was 19. However, he soon left her behind as he pursued his European adventure.

On September 2, 1953, Quincy Jones and Lionel Hampton left New York for Oslo, Norway. The group had high hopes and was not disappointed. Unlike in the United States, in Europe African Americans were taken seriously as artists. In addition, jazz and blues were considered respected musical genres overseas. European audiences gave the band thrilling receptions.

In Stockholm, Quincy also got the chance to compose, arrange, and conduct four songs in a landmark recording session for Art Farmer, Clifford Brown, and the Swedish All-Stars. After the record came out, the word spread like wildfire all over Europe, and in Paris they were asked to record more albums.

The band was extraordinarily busy. It typically performed a concert every evening and sometimes a matinee as well, often traveling a considerable distance between shows. After a concert ended, Quincy frequently stayed up all night working. If he arrived at a recording studio and found more musicians than he had anticipated in the score, Quincy simply wrote additional parts on the spot. Usually,

these sessions were held very late at night or early in the morning. However, Quincy demonstrated he could write anywhere and anytime. In Paris, Jones composed musical pieces for sextets, septets, and octets, (six-, seven-, and eight-piece bands, respectively), and he even wrote music for a 17-piece band that featured both American and French musicians. In Stockholm he wrote for the brass soloist of the Hampton band as well as for a group built around pianist George Wallington. Some of the recordings

European cities, like Stockholm, Sweden, welcomed black musicians and valued jazz as serious music. The enthusiastic reception the band received encouraged Quincy to plunge into composing, arranging, conducting, and recording the band's music.

were made secretly because Gladys Hampton had stipulated that no records could be cut unless all band members were included. Among the recordings made during those moon-lighting sessions were *Quincy Jones and the Swedish All-Stars* and *Stockholm Sweetnin*; these solidified Quincy Jones's reputation as an up-and-coming star among European jazz buffs.

In Paris, Quincy got word from his wife Jeri that she had given birth to a little girl named Jolie. Young and alone in New York, Jeri didn't get to be with Quincy throughout her pregnancy, and the father missed the baby's birth as well as his daughter's early months of life. The couple was apart until Quincy returned to New York. Becoming parents at such a young age, the stress of raising a child, and the strain of Quincy's being on the road put pressure on the marriage. Furthermore, theirs was an interracial union "at a time when that was not the happening thing."

Years later, Jolie Jones Levine recounted an early memory of her father that typifies what life was like for Quincy's wife and daughter: "My mother and I were somewhere waiting for him in a restaurant . . . but he never showed up. I used to say to her, 'Well, I don't know why we're waiting. He's not gonna come!' We just thought he had this genius in him and IT HAD TO BE. Everything else was second, which wasn't so right for us, but that's how it was." Jolie also remembers the days when money was tight and her parents made financial sacrifices to invest in Quincy's future. "It was all about saving in whatever areas they could. Not going to the movies, not having babysitters, so that my father could go down to wherever he had to go to be with the right people, to get where he wanted to go."

Although he loved the thrill of playing on tour, Quincy recognized early in his career that he was not destined to become a leading jazz trumpet soloist. Mixed reviews from other musicians reinforced this realization. Composing and arranging would distinguish Quincy's future more than his

Quincy Jones shares the spotlight with Rashida (left) and Kidada (right), two of his seven children, who were born in the 1970s. In his early years, Quincy always put his career ahead of his family, who sacrificed a great deal to support him in whatever he did. Even though he did not spend very much time with his children while they were growing up, in his heart he loves them very much and speaks of them often with tremendous fatherly pride.

performing, he realized. In an attempt to save the marriage and be a parent to Jolie, Quincy quit the band to work as a freelance music arranger in Manhattan.

Despite Quincy's immaturity and single-minded dedication to his career, he certainly loved his little daughter. Raymond Horricks recalls Quincy in a London restaurant speaking with deep affection about his darling Jolie: "She's a beautiful monster. Only last week we were fast asleep, and she came into the bedroom and switched on our TV. It still didn't wake us. So she got a big packet of crackers and slowly but surely ground them into the bed. Man, you can't sleep on broken biscuits."

New York City's Times Square glistens on a snowy 1950's winter evening. The city was the place to be if Quincy wanted to compose and arrange music, and he soon gained widespread recognition for his arrangements, his collaboration with famous entertainers, and his uncanny ability to spot and develop new recording talent.

4

COMING HOME TO FACE THE MUSIC

IN NEW YORK, Quincy added writing scores for television to his other musical composition and arranging. Much of 1955 was spent shuttling back and forth between his basement apartment on West 59th Street and various recording studios, where Quincy worked on a broad range of musical styles with various artists: gospel singer James Cleveland; Micky Mouse Club Mouseketeer Darlene Gillespie; Jon Hendricks of the jazz vocal trio Lambert, Hendricks, and Ross; trumpeter and saxaphonist Benny Carter; and the blues singers Big Maybelle and Dinah Washington. A new talent that he worked with that year was Julian "Cannonball" Adderley. Quincy's reputation grew with each record.

While arranging scores for big-band leader Tommy Dorsey's summer replacement show on CBS, Quincy met a young singer named Elvis Presley. Dorsey, a trombone player whose band specialized in swing ballads, hated Elvis, but Quincy was drawn to the young man's charisma. During these years, R&B was changing into rock 'n' roll.

41

One day in 1956, Quincy returned home from the studio, and his wife said that Dizzy Gillespie had phoned. "He kept talking about the desert," Jeri reported. Quincy's wife hadn't garbled the message. Gillespie was calling about a proposal from the State Department to sponsor a musical junket through the Middle East and South America. Adam Clayton Powell, an African-American congressman from Harlem, had contacted Gillespie and proposed the musical tour to Congress. The government recognized that bebop was popular abroad, and a goodwill tour would go a long way toward improving America's image.

Happy to escape the tedium of daily recording and eager to travel, Quincy became the trip's organizer. The American National Theatre Academy sent the jazz unit abroad as part of its cultural export program, and the founder of the Institute of Jazz Studies in New York suggested building the band around Dizzy Gillespie—one of the greatest modern trumpeters, who had no band of his own at the time. Quincy was paid well to select band members and rehearse them. (Quincy, who scored some of the music to be played, hadn't touched his trumpet in nearly two years and was busy practicing all the while.) Everyone was enthusiastic, and Jones recalls that all the musicians showed up for rehearsals, even "at the height of a blizzard with arms full of injections"—typhoid shots for traveling overseas.

The group left New York by air and picked up Dizzy in Rome. Quincy recollects, "Once the tour began, Dizzy solidified the band's morale. It was as if a flock of sheep had found its shepherd at last." The group visited Karachi, Pakistan; Beirut, Lebanon; Damascus, Syria; Ankara and Istanbul, Turkey; Belgrade and Zagreb, Yugoslavia; and Athens, Greece. The ensemble included both blacks and whites, men and women. It even played in some countries where women were required to be veiled in public. At the end of a concert in Cypress, Quincy remembers that students who had previously stoned the American Embassy

Quincy was impressed with the style and charisma of the young Elvis Presley, who was a sensation in the mid-1950s. Blending blues and rock, Elvis took the music world by storm and was soon known as the King of Rock 'n' Roll.

now rushed the stage and grabbed Dizzy Gillespie. "We thought we were all in trouble," Quincy relates. But "they put him on their shoulders, and they were cheering him."

In South America, the band went to Quito and Guayaquil, Ecuador; Buenos Aires, Argentina; Montevideo, Uruguay; and a number of cities in Brazil. In the Middle East the climate had been extremely hot; in South America it was winter, and in Quito an altitude of 5,000 feet caused the musicians a shortness of breath while blowing wind instruments. But "music acted like an international language, and people everywhere accepted us on account of it," Quincy observed. "I picked up about twenty words of

Working with jazz trumpeter Dizzy Gillespie (front left), Quincy organized a band tour that included the Middle East and South America. Enthusiastic jazz fans greeted the band everywhere, and the success of the tour added to Quincy's reputation as an organizer and producer.

each language and was really confused at the end of the two tours." Quincy left the band after the South American tour. "I had writing to do, and I wanted to spend some time with my family," he explained.

Back in New York during September of that year, Quincy made his first album as a band leader. An all-star crew of musicians helped Quincy record *This Is How I Feel about Jazz*. The liner notes explained Quincy's reluctance to label the musical style. "I would prefer not to have this music categorized at all for it's probably influenced by every original voice in and outside jazz, maybe anyone from blues singer Ray Charles to Ravel."

In 1957 the excitement of touring had again given way

to the grind of the studio routine. Out of the blue, Quincy was asked to become musical director for Eddie Barclay's label in Paris. A European company, Barclay Disque, was willing to put a black man at the top —which was not the case in the United States in the late 1950s. Quincy took the job, and his work with Barclay Disque in Europe led to awards for conducting and arranging in France, Germany, and Sweden.

While abroad, Quincy made friends with expatriate African-American writers James Baldwin and Richard Wright, as well as the American-born singer Josephine Baker (who worked in France) and Spanish artist Pablo Picasso. At age 25, Quincy studied with the French teacher Nadia Boulanger—a musical and spiritual instructor for some of the world's finest composers, including Aaron Copeland and Leonard Bernstein.

Quincy learned a great deal from Madame Boulanger, even though he was not ready to understand much of what she was trying to teach him at that time in his life. "She told me about principles that I wasn't willing to accept yet, about freedom in music. That you have no freedom until you establish boundaries and parameters," Quincy says. "And she always talked about the power of melody, that melody was king. She just drove that into your head." Years later, Nadia Boulanger would say the two most distinguished pupils she ever taught were Igor Stravinsky and Quincy Jones.

At the start of 1959, few signs would have indicated that the year would become one of the worst in Quincy's life. The previous year, Quincy's old friend Clifford Brown had died in an auto accident. Then what seemed to be a stroke of good luck came Quincy's way. While in New York, arrangements were made for him to meet the producer of a new Broadway show with Pearl Bailey and Al Nicholas. "They wanted me to arrange the score, get my own band—I mean cream band . . . and go to Europe with the show, which was about seventy people— and break the show in, in Holland, Belgium, and France and then meet Sammy Davis, Jr. in London and work the show three weeks there and come back to Broadway and open for two years."

Quincy organized the all-star band to tour Europe with a revival of the Johnny Mercer–Harold Arlen musical *Free and Easy*. The show folded in Paris. Nevertheless, Quincy loved the sound of the ensemble and decided to keep the band together. But Quincy had trouble finding gigs for the band. "I had no management, agents, nothing. I didn't realize what the business side was about, and I had a payroll that I had to come up with every week," Quincy recounts. "I couldn't handle it. I couldn't go on. It was a nightmare just to survive from day to day. That's the closest I ever came in my life to suicide." In the end, Quincy had to sell off rights to his compositions to raise funds. "I had a responsibility to get [the band members home to the States] even if it meant that I'd be in debt for seven years." This ordeal illustrated how much Quincy had yet to learn about the business end of the music industry.

In the early 1960s, there were no African-American executives among the record companies—and few elsewhere in corporate America—so Irvin Green made quite a bold move when he hired Quincy Jones as a talent developer for Mercury Records, then promoted him to vice president in 1962. Quincy worked very hard in his new position: in 1962, he earned his first Grammy Award as a jazz arranger for Count Basie's version of Ray Charles's "I Can't Stop Loving You," and in 1963 he logged 250,000 miles representing Mercury Records in Great Britain, Holland, Italy, and Japan. Quincy performed with Billy Eckstine and added his magic touch to records by Ella Fitzgerald, Sarah Vaughan, and Roland Kirk. Jones also wrote an instrumental version of the score for *Golden Boy*—a Broadway musical set in New York that starred Sammy Davis Jr.

In the spring of 1963, Quincy noticed a demo tape sent to Irvin Green by a Long Island teenager named Leslie Gore. Quincy was impressed by the 16-year-old singer. Within a year, Quincy and Gore brought out a series of top-10 records like "It's My Party," "You Don't Own Me," and "Sunshine and Lollipops"—the first Marvin Hamlisch composition to be recorded. Some critics thought Quincy had "sold out" to pop culture, but Quincy was more than pleased with the work's commercial success.

Paris was the scene of one of Quincy's rare failures when a show with a band he had organized folded in the "City of Lights." In his struggle to keep the band together, he began to realize that he needed more experience in the business end of the music industry.

One of Quincy's most success-
ful collaborations was with
Frank Sinatra, for whom he
arranged many of the singer's
most notable numbers. Sinatra
was awed by Quincy's talents,
and their long relationship
was one of mutual admiration.

At the same time, Quincy was still working with some of the biggest names in jazz and big-band music. In 1964 he produced *It Might as Well Be Swing*, which featured Frank Sinatra and Count Basie. The collaboration was a great success. A year later he put together a Sinatra-Basie show in Las Vegas, conducting the Basie band himself; music from this show was released as *Sinatra at the Sands* in 1966.

Quincy Jones plants a big kiss on longtime friend Tina Sinatra, daughter of Frank Sinatra, at the Frank Sinatra Conference held at Hofstra University in November 1998, after the great singer's death in May of that year. Quincy formed a lasting personal relationship with the Sinatra family during the many years that he worked together with Frank. According to Tina, Quincy was one of the few people that her father truly loved.

Frank Sinatra once said of Quincy Jones: "If I said to Quincy, 'I think the second eight measures don't seem to fit with the mood of the rest of the thing,' he'd go ten feet away and fix it. It always amazed me that a man could do that—to change all of these notes that he had written before." In subsequent years, Sinatra's daughter Tina said of Quincy's relationship with her dad: "My father truly loved very few people, and Quincy Jones was one of them. He is like a brother to me." One Christmas, Tina gave Quincy a replica of Frank Sinatra's famous pinky ring.

When Hollywood beckoned, Quincy left New York and the recording business and began a new career in films. Writing and scoring music for numerous popular and successful films, as well as television, he established himself as one of the most prominent members of the entertainment industry.

5

HOLLYWOOD BECKONS

IN 1965 SIDNEY LUMET, who was married to the daughter of Quincy's good friend Lena Horne, hired Jones to write the score for *The Pawnbroker*—a movie, starring Rod Steiger, about the tragic life of a Holocaust survivor haunted by images of Nazi Germany. Quincy left Mercury Records and New York for Los Angeles.

Lloyd Jones had been delighted with his brother's success in the music industry, so he was flabbergasted that Quincy would leave Mercury Records and take a chance on succeeding in the tough film industry. "When he became the vice president in charge of artists and repertoire of Mercury Records—the first black person to reach that level—I absolutely was so proud," Lloyd said later. "It was just unbelievable. And then he says, " 'I'm going out to Hollywood!' "

However, Quincy's time at Mercury had been difficult for a musician who wasn't cut out for office work. Despite his overwhelming success, he found the regimen distasteful, he later admitted. "I was behind that desk every day . . . awful! You had to be in there at nine o'clock, and you had to wear these Italian suits. You had to fill out expense reports and all that kind of stuff. That really made my skin crawl." Although Quincy had to start all over again in Los Angeles, California's "laid-back" style seemed better suited to his temperament.

Quincy was not just starting over again with his career. His marriage to Jeri had been troubled for years; the couple finally divorced in 1966. Thinking back, Quincy Jones remarked, "I gave up my marriage and I gave up my job. . . . I guess part of it was the adventure and excitement, the danger of jumping into areas you don't really know." His friend Frank Sinatra was in favor of Quincy's move to the West Coast, which he thought might give the musician an entrée into circles that could help him professionally.

After scoring *The Pawnbroker*, Quincy was next hired to write the music for a movie called *Mirage* that starred Gregory Peck. Jones was almost fired when the studio discovered he was black, but Quincy's friend Henry Mancini spoke up and helped him keep the job. By the end of the decade, Jones had scored four films for the noted black actor Sidney Poitier: *In the Heat of the Night*, *For Love of Ivy*, *The Lost Man*, and *Brother John*. Quincy used large orchestras for Goldie Hawn's *Cactus Flower*, and worked on Paul Mazursky's film *Bob & Carol & Ted & Alice*, which dealt with the consequences of wife swapping.

He was also working on music for television. Quincy wrote the theme song for NBC's *Ironside*, a 1960s television series about a detective in a wheelchair. This assignment marked the first time a synthesizer was used in a TV score. In 1970 Quincy wrote the theme song for Bill Cosby's first sitcom on NBC.

As he became established in Hollywood, Quincy started spending time among the rich and famous members of the film and television industry. On New Year's Eve 1967, for example, he was at Michael Caine's house in London with Roman Polanski and wife Sharon Tate. There, Billy Eckstine introduced Quincy to Jesse Jackson, who was at that

time an aide to Dr. Martin Luther King Jr.

In 1968, after Dr. King was assassinated, Quincy went back home to Chicago. Overwhelmed by the tension and anger of the period, he sought out Jackson. Under the Civil Rights leader's guidance, Jones became increasingly involved with civic and political causes. In 1972 Quincy Jones helped Jesse Jackson organize Black EXPO, an annual event sponsored by the black business communities of America, in Chicago to raise awareness and money for Jackson's Operation PUSH (People United to Save Humanity). In 1973, Jones spearheaded the Institute for Black American Music (IBAM). He also organized a Black Arts Festival that included concerts and musical seminars to support a natural art and music library for members of the black community. (Quincy would eventually donate money to Jesse Jackson when the activist minister decided

From left to right, Sammy Davis Jr., Harry Belafonte, and Sidney Poitier share a moment in Las Vegas with Quincy in 1970. In Hollywood, Quincy worked closely with African-American actors and entertainers, such as Poitier, for whom he scored several films.

to campaign for the Democratic presidential nomination in 1984 and again in 1988.)

Working in Hollywood turned out to be a trying, though gratifying, affair for Quincy. In the beginning, the time between movie assignments proved excessive. As Quincy put it, "I just don't know if I can wait that long between meals." Later, when film jobs came more frequently, the work was demanding. "I was doing up to eight movies a year. . . . I must have done thirty-four, thirty-eight films," Quincy noted with exhaustion.

Some people consider Quincy's masterpiece his music for the film version of Truman Capote's *In Cold Blood*, but even this job did not come easily. The studio and Capote wanted Leonard Bernstein to write the score, and Quincy himself agreed with them. But Richard Brooks, who directed the film and wrote the screenplay, wanted Quincy.

The book and film dealt with the particularly brutal murders of a Kansas farming family, the Clutters, committed by two deranged ex-convicts, Perry Smith and Dick Hickock. Based on a real incident Capote researched, the book and later the script gave Quincy an opportunity to use music to depict psychological material. The score became an integral part of the characters' minds and their motivation, not just background for the action. As with *The Pawnbroker*, this music dealt with serious, violent subject matter in contrast to the pastoral life of the Clutters—before their innocent lives were shattered. Light, trite tunes were not appropriate. In preparation for writing the music, Quincy received tapes from Richard Brooks from the interrogation of the murderers. "That's where the score came from," he acknowledged.

Steven Spielberg later said, "Quincy wrote one of the best movie scores I'd ever heard for *In Cold Blood*. When I was seventeen years old, I made a film in college, and I tracked the entire picture with the *In Cold Blood* score." Predictions were that Quincy would win an Academy Award in 1967. That year, Jones was honored with two Oscar nominations for songs from *For Love of Ivy* and *The Eyes of Love*, but

neither won; no mention was made of the music for *In Cold Blood*. In an interview with Herb Nolan of *Down Beat*, Quincy described the problem of composing music for movies, in contrast to records:

> If you are writing for a record, be it three minutes or ten, it has an organic unity that takes care of itself because it exists for the sake of the music. But in films, when you are playing outside of a scene in a third dimension to create an atmosphere, you are dealing with a wholly different abstract form. The film dictates all the form for you. . . . In movies you come in after there's dialogue, photography, interpretation, direction and lighting, so you are coming in with pre-established, pre-conceived dramatic direction. You can't fight it. The music is just one of the elements, which is hard to live with over a period of time.

Because of such frustration, Quincy was overjoyed to

Following the assassination of Martin Luther King Jr. (standing on his motel balcony just prior to being shot, second from right), Quincy became actively involved in the civil rights movement. He worked with Jesse Jackson (shown here to the left of King) and other African-American leaders to organize and promote business and cultural events to benefit the black community.

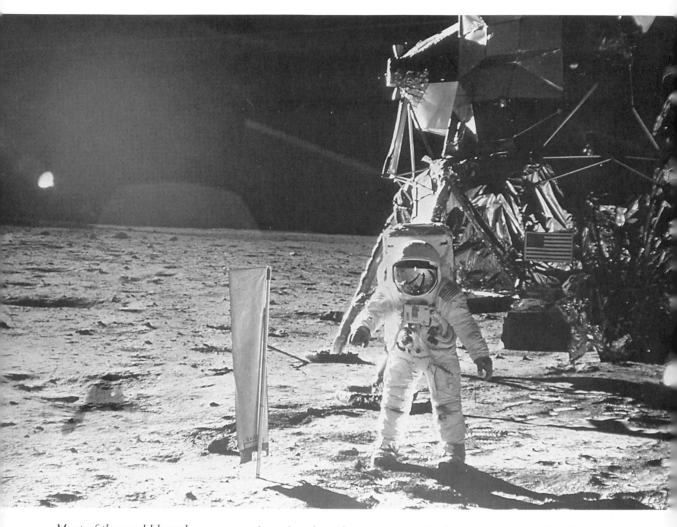

Most of the world heard Quincy's arrangement of "Fly Me to the Moon" when the Apollo 11 astronauts played the song upon landing on the moon in July 1969.

take a break and accept a musical assignment unrelated to film. In 1969, Jones went to New York and in 10 days wrote and recorded the album *Walking in Space*. This record later won a Grammy for Best Jazz Performance by a Group. When astronauts Neil Armstrong and Buzz Aldrin landed on the moon in 1969, Aldrin played Quincy's arrangement of "Fly Me to the Moon"—giving worldwide exposure to the song.

Among the other varied activities to which Jones committed himself in Hollywood was a 1973 CBS special titled *Duke Ellington . . . We Love You Madly*. In creating this TV extravaganza, Quincy worked as composer, arranger, conductor, contractor, producer, and even sound technician at times. Others who participated included, Peggy Lee, Sarah Vaughan, Roberta Flack, Aretha Franklin, Count Basie, Louis Bellson, Harry Carney, Sammy Davis Jr., Billy Eckstine, and Joe Williams.

In order to produce at the level Quincy Jones has achieved throughout his life, a grueling work schedule is required. Even though Quincy loves what he does, the hours he devotes to his career are extensive. "It's that constant need to create and move that keeps me going. I get up at six and go on permanently non-stop until midnight, with occasional meal-breaks if there's time. It'll continue until one day I'm stopped. I could never imagine myself not working because my work is a labor of love, totally. If one day my love for it all starts to wear thin, then maybe I'll decide to hang it up—but, believe me, I doubt that time will ever come."

Whenever Quincy throws himself into a new project, he follows a punishing schedule and does much of his writing at night. Calling himself "the Phantom of Brentwood," Quincy explains that he "can hear better at night. The phone doesn't ring. . . . But the real reason I write and arrange at such weird hours is the psychological effect it has on being creative. After you get past a certain point, your subconscious mind comes out. It breaks through all your artistic fears and inhibitions. You start to dream while you're still awake. Maybe it's what you would call hallucinating." Quincy has been known to go three or four nights without sleep when working on projects like the Duke Ellington show. He credits self-discipline as his secret. Despite such hours, Quincy does not have a studio in his house. "I never wanted a studio in my home," he says. "A lot of people have it, but I think a studio is a very sacred place. And I don't want to be wandering around in my underwear at three o'clock in the morning in there. That's not very sacred."

Lloyd Jones described the way his brother works: "I don't know if you've ever seen him write, but he gets his head kind of cocked as if the notes were stabbing him in the back. The only way you could really get to him was to hit a chord in a different key."

The devotion Quincy Jones gave to his work was at the expense of loved ones. His personal life suffered. In 1966, one year after moving to California, Quincy's second daughter, Tina, was born. That same year, Jeri Jones and Quincy divorced. In 1967, Quincy married Ulla Anderson, and the next year Ulla gave birth to son Quincy Delight Jones III (later called QDIII). But Quincy later said of that union: "I wasn't in any better shape for the second marriage. Probably just trying to create that nest again." Quincy and Ulla officially divorced in 1974.

Deeper than any tendency to bottle up feelings was self-centeredness and an inability to accept limits. Like jazz, friendship has a certain degree of improvisation, but in a marital context Quincy had more trouble with commitment than spontaneity. Likewise, Quincy made friends with ease and found plenty of brides. He had yet to learn that compromise, devotion to children's needs, and loyalty to one person demand the same kind of passion he reserved for music. It would be many more years before Quincy realized family life, like music, is an art; success is dependent upon the amount of time and energy invested.

Quincy had never come to terms with his father's treatment of his mother, which probably interfered with Quincy's own ability to establish a lasting marriage. As a child, Quincy blamed his mother for leaving but didn't question his father's conduct in abandoning a sick wife and carrying on with other women. Without the role model of a father to teach Quincy how to love and respect a wife, he had difficulty sharing his life with a woman and accepting the limitations marriage entails. In addition, the fact that six of Quincy's children were daughters (he had only one son) may have complicated matters. Unresolved aspects of Quincy's

feelings toward his mother compromised his relationships with *all* women. As is often the case with such tragedies, victims of neglect revisit their own traumas on the next generation. Because Quincy felt neglected by his mother, he may have handled this hurt subconsciously by emotionally abandoning the women in his life—including those "little women" who needed him most.

Jolie tells a story of her father coming to visit school but ignoring her because he was engrossed in work. "He came once, when I was in junior high, to spend some time at the school. I guess he had an arrangement that wasn't done. He was in the back of my classroom writing an arrangement. You know, you kind of just wished that Dad would just come and watch your stuff." Although Jolie Jones Levine

Listening with headphones as he scribbles the music, Quincy is a workaholic when he is involved in a project. His passionate devotion to his work has over the years played havoc with his personal life, particularly his relationships with women and with his children.

Surrounded by his family, Quincy speaks to the audience at the Quincy Jones Tribute in 1997. Although estranged from his loved ones over the years, he came to realize that he had to give the same devotion and loyalty to his family that he has given to his music.

later remarked, "His heart was always there, and I know that now," she doesn't appear to have known it when she was a small girl and needed her father's attention.

Quincy often spoke of his musical counterparts in familial terms. "It was a big, big family. The whole big band thing was about a family." Although this statement indicates Jones's need for a sense of family, which the bands obviously provided, it also shows a displacement onto work of family feeling that belonged at home. Quincy may well have been projecting some of his loyalty to kin onto professional colleagues, which could have contributed to the repeated marital breakups in his actual family.

Quincy says about neglecting his offspring: "I've taken a lot of time from my children that should have been their time in order to put it into my creative outlet. And it feels selfish to me now, and I've got to do something about it while I have the time."

In Hollywood, Quincy met the woman who would become his third wife: a blond ex-model turned actress who appeared on television frequently. Peggy Lipton was particularly well known from the television show *Mod Squad*. "She's my greatest source of inspiration," Quincy said of Lipton. "She's smart, compassionate, imaginative, creative, she writes music and stories, and she never hassles me."

In 1974, everything seemed to be going wonderfully for Quincy. His new album, *Body Heat*, was selling better than any other album in his career, and he was dating a great new woman. The only signs of trouble on the horizon were throbbing, lingering headaches. At 41, Quincy Jones had no reason to believe that his life might soon come to an end.

Quincy's career was interrupted and almost came to an end when in 1974 he suffered a severe stroke. His brush with death helped give him insight into his own feelings as he explained that ". . . you realize you're very insignificant in the scheme of things."

6

AT DEATH'S DOOR

WHILE MAKING *BODY HEAT,* Quincy felt tired and had headaches, but he attributed these symptoms to overwork. However, disaster struck during the summer of 1974 in the form of a cerebral stroke. It was an extremely warm afternoon in August when Quincy and his girlfriend Peggy were resting together. Quincy had been talking when suddenly he grew quiet. Peggy noticed Quincy had slumped over on the pillow, and his face was contorted with pain. An aneurysm—a bubble-like defect in the carotid artery that supplies blood to the right side of the brain—had ruptured inside Quincy's head, spilling blood into the base of the brain.

Quincy described the intense pain as follows: "It felt like somebody had shot off the back of my head. I'd never felt anything like it in my life, and after a while it seemed as if I could actually hear and feel the blood sloshing around in there. It was like the life was actually leaking out of my body. I could feel death. I wasn't ready to go, but I could sense, just in a flash, what it would be like not being here. I began thinking of my youngest daughter who was just a baby and didn't even know me yet. *I just wasn't ready to go.*"

Dr. Elsie A. Giorgi, an Italian physician, rushed to Quincy's home and immediately diagnosed the problem. Dr. Giorgi stayed with Quincy, preparing him so that life-saving surgery could be performed. When he arrived at the hospital, Quincy's head was shaved. Indelible ink marked off the area where the skull would be opened to reveal the brain.

The type of stroke Quincy had suffered was more complicated than the average stroke. Two operations were required, and the chances of surviving the second were only one in a hundred. (In 1973 kung-fu champion and actor Bruce Lee died from an aneurysm, and in 1965 actress Patricia Neal suffered brain damage after such a rupture.) The doctors informed Quincy that he might die and had him sign papers indicating what to do with his body. Yet Quincy was determined to live.

Quincy's aneurysm was caused by a weak spot in the wall of the artery. Quincy was born with this common defect, which sometimes does little more than cause occasional headaches for people with the problem. For others, years of pressure from blood surging through the artery causes the weak spot to grow thinner. Blowouts are usually fatal. Upon rupturing, aneurysms kill more than a third of their victims, but fortunately in Quincy's case, the artery involved lay *against* the brain, not deep within it, and the blood vessel did not burst, it was slowly leaking blood.

Preoperative tests revealed Quincy could live for several days without surgery. However, these tests also showed that Quincy had a similar aneurysm in a blood vessel on the other side of his brain. This one was not yet ready to tear; still, it was potentially dangerous. Within three months, the same operation would have to be performed again on the other side of his brain. The chances of Quincy Jones surviving both procedures were slim.

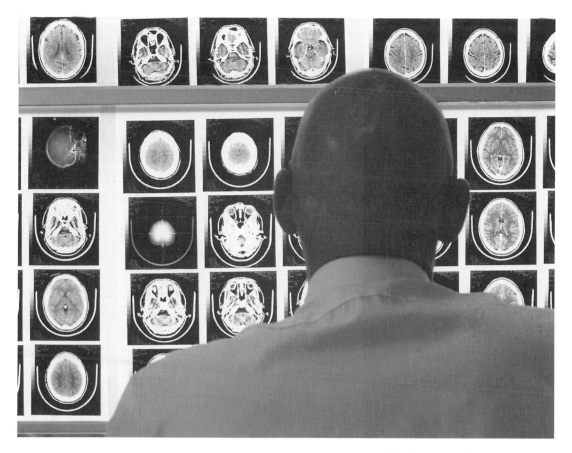

Dr. Giorgi nearly closed her Beverly Hills practice to supervise every detail of Quincy Jones's medical case over the next few weeks. For the first operation, the surgical team consisted of Dr. Marshall Grode (who had performed brain surgery on singer Stevie Wonder following a 1973 car crash) and Dr. Milton D. Heifetz (author of *The Right to Die* and inventor of the widely-used "Heifetz Clip" used for trapping aneurysms and rendering them harmless). Massive doses of cortisone were given to Quincy to lower his blood pressure and reduce swelling in the brain.

Quincy Jones underwent seven hours of surgery in which an incision was made in his head from behind the right eye to behind the right ear. Then the scalp was drawn back, holes were drilled in the skull, and a large

To discover and correct a brain trauma such as Quincy's, doctors studied a series of brain images. Although the damage was life threatening, Quincy beat the odds and survived two operations.

Quincy's third wife, Peggy Lipton, was at his side through his operations and painful recovery. Here the couple display the star Quincy received from being part of the Hollywood Walk of Fame in 1980.

semicircular piece of skull was removed using a special saw. The inch of damaged artery was repaired, a Heifetz Clip was put in place, and then a metal plate covered the gaping hole. Quincy survived the surgery.

The next month, in September, the recovering musician/producer married Peggy Lipton in a ceremony performed at her parents' Los Angeles home. In October, Quincy had a second operation. This time, the neurosurgeon from the first procedure, Dr. Grode, and Dr. Charles Carlton (who had operated on Patricia Neal) opened the left side of Quincy's head. Again, the operation was completely successful.

. Later, Quincy did some research and learned that the odds against coming through just *one* of the operations were four to one. Up to 90 percent of all brain surgery patients suffer complications that can either kill them or leave them paralyzed, blind, or unable to talk. Quincy realized just one slip of either one of the surgeons' knives—even just a millimeter—and he would have ended up as a "vegetable" or dead. Right after they finished operating on him, the surgeons took a black physician in for the same operation, and he died on the table. This forced Quincy to say, "You have to stand back and look at your life and see if you've got your priorities right."

Philosophically, Quincy understands his survival this way:

> A lot of people were praying for me, and God just wasn't ready for me yet. But you still have to fight to come through. The doctors told me they could do about 30 percent of what it took for me to stick around, but the rest was up to me. I remember when I came out of the anaesthesia that second time and I wanted to jump out of bed and yell: 'Wow, I made it again. I'm still here!' That's how great I felt about being alive. And when you feel like that, you've got to start looking at everything in a different light. . . . You look at everything, even a blade of grass, and you realize you're really very insignificant in the scheme of things.

The first noticeable aftereffects of the surgery were occasional lapses of memory and weakness, but Quincy rapidly overcame both problems. In fact, the hardest part of recovery was staying out of his studio.

Following Quincy's brush with death, he changed in other ways. Charles Saunders of *Ebony* magazine related a tale Quincy told him about returning to work. Jones had an argument with a man he knew before the surgery, and for the first time Quincy cursed at the fellow. The guy was surprised because Quincy had always seemed like such an easygoing person. In good humor, Quincy later explained, "So he phoned my doctor and said: 'Hey! Did y'all leave

some of this n———'s brain on the operating floor?'"
Quincy continued:

> I haven't turned mean or anything like that, but I don't ever
> again intend to hold all my feelings inside and refuse to get
> things out into the open. There's no more *pretending* about
> anything. If I don't like somebody, then I'm not going to
> have anything to do with him. . . . I don't care anymore
> about the non-essential, the phony . . . things in life—
> money, fame, the big houses and cars. Man, when they had
> my head open, none of those things meant *anything*, and
> ever since then some of my old values have been turned
> upside down.

Quincy is very aware of how others treat him as well as
how he treats others. Recently he was in an airport when
the metal in his skull triggered the alarm. He explained to
the guard about his operation. The man asked Quincy to
remove his hat so his head could be examined. When the
guard announced he saw no evidence of metal, it was all
Quincy could do to restrain himself. "I was mad, but all
I said was: 'Fool, it ain't up under my hat; it's inside my
head!'"

Quincy also has to avoid microwave ovens because the
metal plates could become hot and scorch his brain,
according to Saunders. But most painful was when Quincy
was told he could not play the trumpet. The pressure
required to make music on the instrument—especially high
notes—could burst the strained blood vessels in his brain
and kill him almost instantly.

Quincy's trumpet was a gift from Dizzy Gillespie—the
first horn ordered from the manufacturer with the bell
turned up. It had been one of Quincy's most cherished pos-
sessions since the jazz star gave it to him in 1956. Quincy
didn't really believe the doctors, so shortly after the second
operation he tried playing the slide trumpet. "I heard the
thing start to crackle and pop, and I haven't touched the
horn since," he said.

In a 1995 article for the *Los Angeles Times*, Bruce Newman compared Quincy's inability to play his instrument to the great composer Beethoven's deafness. "With his right hand, Quincy Jones lifts the trumpet from the dark velvet lining of the case in which it has been entombed for twenty years," Newman wrote. "Then with practiced ease he puts the mouthpiece delicately to his lips. He takes a breath and holds it for a measure, thinks about the note that he would blow and the likelihood that blowing it would kill him dead, pulls the horn away and holds the note in his head."

During the 1980s, Quincy continued his success as he organized tours and events, collaborated with other musicians, and produced hit records as well as music for films and television shows. His hectic schedule took its toll, however, and by the end of the decade, his personal life was again in turmoil.

7

CLIMBING THE MOUNTAIN AND FALLING OFF

BEFORE THE OPERATIONS to correct his aneurysms, Quincy had been working hard on compositions using electronic, synthesizer-based music. In the 1960s and 1970s, African-American musicians began replacing lyrics about love and dancing with songs dealing with social themes. At the same time, Third World influences—including congas, bongos, and kalimba—were becoming popular, and instruments such as the Moog synthesizer, wahwah pedals for guitars, and the electric piano changed the sound of modern music.

With respect to electronic elements, Quincy recommended moderation in amplification as well as other features. "For me, electronics are just another instrument in the orchestra, like an extra clarinet player. It's another tone or color. Naturally, you have to use it like garlic salt. You just can't slam it all around the place."

Early in 1975, Quincy felt recovered from his surgery and began making plans for a tour of Japan to launch his new album, *Mellow Madness*. Quincy took on two new players, Louis and George Johnson.

Author Alex Haley, whose story of his ancestors became the epic television drama Roots, *asked Quincy to write the music for the production. Using a great deal of original African music, Quincy's score was a tremendous hit and exposed millions of viewers to the musical heritage of African Americans.*

The fellows couldn't read music and feared they'd embarrass themselves in front of the well-known producer, but Quincy took them under his wing—as Ray Charles and Clark Terry had done for him many years back. The tour to Japan went well, and while traveling Quincy offered a crash course in music theory. The Johnsons, in turn, contributed four songs to *Mellow Madness*. The Johnson brothers (they recorded as the Brothers Johnson) had written over 200 compositions, and Quincy signed them to A&M Records. Their debut album, *Look Out for Number 1,* was a great success. When it sold more than a million copies in 1976, it became the first platinum album produced by Quincy Jones.

That year was a good one personally as well: Peggy and Quincy had their second daughter, Rashida, in 1976.

At around this time, Jones was asked to write the music for a television miniseries, *Roots*, written by Alex Haley. Haley and Jones had been friends since the days when Quincy was at Mercury Records in New York. Haley's monumental work traced the journey of his ancestors from Africa to America, including their struggles during slavery and its aftermath. A personalized approach to African-Amerian history, the programs ran over several successive nights on TV.

Quincy's music for *Roots* incorporated African chants, although the producers restricted him from using as much original material as he would have liked. Nevertheless, this was the first time American audiences were exposed to the source of black musical heritage en masse. Jones later explained:

> African music had always been regarded in the West as primitive and savage, but when you take the time to really study it, you see that it's as structured and sophisticated as European classical music, with the same basic components as you'll find in an symphony orchestra—instruments that are plucked, instruments that are beaten, and instruments that are blown with reeds. And it's music from the soil— powerful, elemental. . . . From gospel, blues, jazz, soul, R&B, rock 'n' roll, all the way to rap, you can trace the roots straight back to Africa.

Roots was an incredible success. Audiences were deeply moved, and the series received the highest ratings ever in television viewing.

Quincy and Michael Jackson with their Grammy awards. His work with Michael on the latter's album Thriller *was one of Quincy's biggest successes, earning the duo seven singles in the top 10 and selling millions of copies.*

The next year, Quincy scored *The Wiz*—Universal Studio's all-black musical version of *The Wizard of Oz*. This project was brought to Quincy by director Sidney Lumet. Quincy did a fine job, although he wasn't fond of the music from the original Broadway show or the script. Quincy produced the film at Michael Jackson's request, but it was not a commercial success. However, the producer did enjoy working with Michael Jackson. "Before we started on the film, Michael came over to the house for rehearsal," Quincy recalled. "I'll never forget that. He was so cute, so shy. . . . He really impressed me because he was only nineteen years old then I couldn't believe his comprehension. I began to feel that there was something inside of him that I had never heard before on the records." Well before their collaboration on *Thriller*, the recording that would go on to become the best-selling album of all time, Quincy Jones predicted, "Michael Jackson is going to be one of the biggest stars of the eighties and nineties."

Quincy had more work than he could possibly do by the mid-1980s. He left A&M Records and formed his own label, Qwest, in 1980. Among the first hits he produced on the new label was the single "Baby, Come to Me," featuring his protégés James Ingram and Patti Austin. "Baby, Come to Me" quickly climbed to number one on the pop music charts in 1982. That same year Quincy won a Grammy as Producer of the Year for his 1981 album *The Dude,* and another Grammy for a recording of Lena Horne's Broadway show. Domestic tranquility seemed to be reflected in his dedication of *The Dude* to: "My wife Peggy; my children Jolie, Tina, Quincy III, Kidada, and Rashida; plus my grandchildren Donovan and Sonny; to my favorite singer and the daughter I don't recall asking for, Patti Austin."

But it was another project in 1982 that would turn out to be the biggest success for Quincy Jones. When Michael Jackson's album *Thriller* was released that year, it redefined popular music. Quincy had worked with Michael on all of the musical details of the album. Their work paid off with seven top-10 singles and an unprecedented 41 million copies sold worldwide.

Quincy kept producing one hit after another. The song "We Are the World" was recorded in 1985 to raise money for famine relief in Ethiopia. Shortly after the American Music Awards that year, 45 of the biggest names in pop

Quincy poses in front of some of his award-winning records. The records he produced under his own label quickly moved to the top of the pop-music charts and kept him in the ranks of award winners.

music gathered at the Lion Share and A&M Studios in Los Angeles to record this song, by Michael Jackson and Lionel Richie, including such superstars as Bruce Springsteen, Stevie Wonder, Paul Simon, Diana Ross, Bob Dylan, Billy Joel, Kenny Rogers, Cyndi Lauper, Smokey Robinson, Sheila E, the Pointer Sisters, and Willie Nelson. Quincy Jones was selected to produce the single.

It was "a terrifying responsibility," Quincy said, "because it's just enormous, an enormous canvas." All the people involved were "very original, soulful individuals," according to Quincy—but this, of course, did not necessarily make them easy to work with. To make things even harder, only one recording session could be devoted to the single; there would be no time for retakes. Because of this, Quincy made it clear to the stars that he would be in charge. As each person arrived, Quincy told him or her, "Leave your ego right there at the door." Actually, the recording session went quite smoothly, largely because of Quincy Jones's ability to calm everyone's nerves and organize the group. The single was distributed by CBS Records and earned more than $200 million, more than any other single in history.

The success of *Thriller* and "We Are the World" solidified Quincy Jones's position as pop's premier producer. Next he turned his talents to producing movies, starting with a film based on Alice Walker's novel *The Color Purple*, which recounts the story of two black sisters in the South victimized by racism and male chauvinism. Quincy coproduced the film and asked Steven Spielberg to direct. Quincy's choice of a white director disturbed many people—even Spielberg himself, initially. The director of *E.T.,* a children's fantasy about an extraterrestrial visitor, may not have seemed a natural choice. When Speilberg voiced his reservations, Quincy asked, "Did you have to go to outer space and hire a superior intelligence to direct a movie about an alien?"

Jones chose Oprah Winfrey, who was relatively unknown at the time, to play Sophia in *The Color Purple*. Jones spotted Oprah on her local television talk show when he was visiting Chicago, and the film launched Oprah's subsequent rise to fame. Oprah credits Quincy with giving her emotional support during the filming: "I don't think I would have gotten through it had he not been there, because it was undoubtedly the most intimidating experience I've ever had."

The Color Purple also lifted the career of comedian Whoopi Goldberg, and Quincy himself wrote the score.

When it was released in 1985, the film received good reviews.

Professionally, Quincy Jones was on top, with one success after another. He had become phenomenally wealthy thanks to his artistic achievements. But his personal life was not going so well: his marriage to Peggy Lipton was crumbling. Daughter Jolie Jones Levine observed, "He didn't see things coming until they were right on top of him." From the perspective of a child of divorce, Jolie knew the pain these breakups cost. "The life just went right out of the house. I know it happened each time. . . . The phone stops ringing, people don't come over any more."

Oprah Winfrey offered a gentle observation of why the marriage failed: "I think he really belongs to the world. As a woman, you have to know that. You have to feel that he is not really all yours and could never be. The price which that extracts in a relationship is a very heavy one."

Quincy took the breakup from Peggy Lipton very hard. With considerable insight he observed:

> These last three years have been killing [me]. It has been the best and worst of times. I've been playing out a lot of crazy dreams and doing a lot of reflecting. I had been moving so fast that I never looked over my shoulder. I think that now I'm beginning to grow up. Over three marriages and thirty-five years, I could always depend on someone else to take care of me. I don't drive, and I don't cook. Suddenly, I was by myself and I had thousands of decisions to make. Here I was, fifty-three, and like a kid who couldn't take care of myself. I had to dig down deep and start trying to take responsibility for my life.

Quincy's despair was complicated by exhaustion from overwork, and a full-scale nervous breakdown seemed to be on the horizon. A doctor told Quincy "you've got problems," and helped him to recognize he needed "time out." Jones ran away to Tahiti and let nature's tropical paradise—on a Pacific island owned by Marlon Brando—start to heal him.

Established as the premier pop-music producer, Quincy continued to earn honors. Here, he holds three Grammys he received in 1982 for his musical achievements.

As coproducer of the film The Color Purple, *Quincy chose a relative unknown, Oprah Winfrey, for a leading role, helping to launch her to future stardom. When she won the 1997 People's Choice Award for Favorite Female in a Television Series, Quincy presented her with the award and a loving hug and kiss.*

Daughter Jolie recounts that family members gradually came to understand the depth of Quincy's disturbance. "I didn't realize how heavy it was. I don't think anybody did, until he had to go away." Similarly, correspondence from the South Seas indicated Jones was not himself. "It was a strange postcard," said Jolie about a note she received from her dad. "He told us how much he missed us, how much he loved us, and that he'd been trying to write this card for ten days. And I . . . I thought, 'Boy,' you know, 'he must really be having a hard time.'"

In Tahiti, Quincy spent his days communing with nature, observing the simple life of the natives, and grieving the end of his relationship. Quincy had to come to terms with a tremendous loss in his life that was the direct result of his own behavior. At one point Quincy felt he had had a mystical experience in which he saw a vision. "A whole tunnel opened up in the sky, and it was white and gold, and it went all the way up to heaven," he later explained. "It was really scary. My soul left my body over there. Phew! It really did, man! I swear to God!" A psychologist might interpret the dreamlike imagery of Quincy's vision as a symbol of enlightenment or an afterlife. Quincy seemed to be looking for a sign of hope that loss need not be inevitable, that immortality was possible.

Holding yet another well-deserved award, Quincy shares the spotlight with son Quincy III. In his later years, Quincy has found satisfaction and contentment after a long career of outstanding accomplishments in promoting many styles of music and developing the talents of so many music artists and entertainers.

8

HARVESTING
THE FRUITS OF
ONE'S LABOR

WHEN QUINCY RETURNED to the United States, he tried to
reconnect with his children. In fact, a present he gave to son Quincy
III (whom he called "Snoopy") was the starting point for the first
album Jones had made in a decade. Snoopy, who was raised in Sweden,
was wild about rap. For the boy's 17th birthday, Quincy took him out
to meet some of the biggest rap stars in the country. "My son just
adored these guys," said the 56-year-old producer. "His thrill at meeting these rappers reminded me of when I was his age and I first came
to New York in the late '40s with Oscar Pettiford, and met Bird and
Miles and Mingus and Monk. I was so overwhelmed that I almost
couldn't handle it."

Rap manager Russell Simmons helped set up the meeting, and both
Quincys dined with the rap artists at Canastel's—a chic Italian restaurant on Park Avenue South in Manhattan. L.L.Cool J, the Beastie Boys,
Whodini and the Fat Boys, Oran (Juice), Kurtis Blow, and Run-D.M.C.
showed up for this momentous encounter. Quincy identified with the

young musicians' contempt for racism, authority, and conventionality. He recognized the connections between the beboppers of one generation and the hip-hoppers of another.

In 1988 and 1989, Quincy worked on his new album *Back on the Block*. It began with some raps written by Quincy Jones Jr. and Quincy Jones III: father and son performed together. The title song combines lyrics by Ice-T, Melle Mel, Big Daddy Kane, and Kool Moe Dee. Performed by a multigenerational group of artists, the album contains selections from Quincy's entire career, showing the evolution of his style and the musical tradition from which it came. The idea of using the voice as an instrument is illustrated in songs like "Wee B. Dooinit." In one section, the sounds Quincy made on his body—beating his chest, scratching his head—were run through an enhancer and used as drums and shakers. Swahili lyrics, synthesizers, and choirs lend diversity and reach to the album. "I wanted to make an album that incorporated the whole family of American black music from gospel to jazz, everything that's part of my culture," said Quincy.

In 1990 the biographical film *Listen Up: The Lives of Quincy Jones* was produced by Courtney Sale Ross. (A book by the same title was also published.) In 1991, Quincy became coproducer of the Montreux Jazz and World Music Festival. He also helped launch NBC-TV's hit series *The Fresh Prince of Bel Air*, for which he was the executive producer. The soundtrack album for *Boyz N the Hood* was released in 1991.

The following year, Quincy developed *VIBE* magazine and directed 85 black performers in a spectacular performance: *Handel's Messiah: A Soulful Celebration*. Although Quincy doesn't seem to be terribly religious in the traditional sense of that term, he has remarked that "a person who doesn't believe in a higher power" has to think twice when "there are too many things that come together for it just to be an accident." Quincy also referred to divine intervention when speaking of artistic freedom: "There

Quincy attends a gala with actress Nastassja Kinski. Like so many of Quincy's relationships with women, the liaison did not last, and the couple split after the birth of their daughter.

is an expression I always use in the studio: you have to leave room for God to walk through the door."

In January 1993 Quincy produced the inaugural concert at the Lincoln Memorial for President Clinton. Working with David Salzman, Quincy mounted "An American Reunion" of great music, which was televised nationally on HBO (Home Box Office). Also in 1993, *Miles and Quincy Live at Montreux* came out, featuring Miles Davis along

The young comedian Sinbad is introduced by Quincy as the host of the late-night talk show Vibe, *another of Quincy's television projects for which he was the executive producer.*

with Quincy Jones. David Salzman and Quincy Jones merged their companies in 1993 to form QDE: Quincy Jones and David Salzman Entertainment, a co-venture with Time Warner, Inc. Quincy became co-CEO and chairman.

On the personal front, in 1993 Quincy's daughter Kenya Julia Miambi Sarah was born to actress Nastassja Kinski. The child was Nastassja's third and Quincy's seventh. Quincy was present for the birth at Cedars Sinai Hospital in Los Angeles. Before long, however, Quincy and Nastassja split up, after which Quincy became involved with Mickella Tupta.

In 1994, Quincy narrated the documentary *A Great Day*

in Harlem. Nominated for an Academy Award, this film tells the story of how photographer Art Kane assembled 57 of the finest jazz musicians for a picture in August of 1958, taken in front of a Harlem brownstone, for publication in *Esquire* magazine. The documentary features interviews with 30 musical greats like Dizzy Gillespie, Sonny Rollins, and Art Blakey; rare archival footage of performances by Cab Callaway; and home movies from the period.

In 1995, QDE released a CD-ROM history of music: *479 A.D. to Today*, in which a spirit named "Q" leads listeners through time. Also in 1995, Quincy became the executive producer of a late-night variety show called *Mad TV*. In 1996 Quincy produced the Academy Awards show and telecast. Between 1997 and 1998, he was executive producer for the syndicated talk show *Vibe* and in 1998 published *Blaze*—a magazine devoted to hip-hop music and culture.

Although he was involved in so many projects, Quincy was not neglecting music. During the late 1980s, several albums of his jazz material were released, including *Classics, Vol. 3* and *Strike up the Band*. Qwest released his album *Q's Jook Joint* in 1995, which netted Quincy the NAACP Image Award for Best Jazz Artist. "*Q's Jook Joint* blends the latest in hip-hop flavored productions with sleek urban ballads, vintage standards, and derivative pieces; everything's superbly crafted," wrote music reviewer Ron Wynn.

His next album was never intended to be released; he originally created the collection of 26 favorite love songs for his own enjoyment and as a gift for his friend Oprah Winfrey. "I love Oprah and wanted to share something with her," he explained. "So I had this printed up and her picture put on the front with a warm dedication. Then her friends said, 'I'd like to get some of these.' So after a while, everybody started pressuring me to put it out." *From Q with Love* was released by Qwest in 1999.

Although the album had been made with Winfrey in mind, it was dedicated to Quincy's brother Lloyd, who had died in 1998, and Lloyd's wife Gloria. In the liner notes to the album, Quincy wrote:

> It was during my Las Vegas gig with Sinatra at the Sands Hotel in 1966 that I invited Lloyd to be with me as I conducted and arranged for the great Count Basie Band (Frank's backing band at the time). Starting with Chicago in the '30s, Lloyd and I grew up hungry together, slept together, struggled together and dreamt together. More than any other person in the world, he appreciated how far we'd come to that moment. He fell in love with a beautiful woman that night (and vice-versa), and they loved each other for thirty-two years until his dying breath.

A photograph of Quincy and his "baby brother" that had been taken in Chicago in 1936 came with the album.

In 1999 Quincy's mother died. These were difficult losses. He had also suffered family heartbreak a few years earlier, when rapper Tupac Shakur was killed in a drive-by shooting in September 1996. The musician had been engaged to Quincy's daughter Kidada, an actress and a model. For a long time, Quincy had been concerned about the escalation of violence both within the African-American community and across the country in general. Tragically, he learned that even his own family could be touched by the grim losses associated with guns.

Over the course of his long career, Quincy Jones has been the recipient of many well-deserved honors—a list of which would fill pages of this book. He has received more than 80 Grammy Awards for his music. In 1990, Quincy won the French *Legion d'Honneur*. In 1994 he was given the Polar Music Prize in Stockholm, Sweden. Quincy donated the cash award of $128,000 to the African National Congress. Also that year, Jones served on the board of a six-hour hunger relief telethon held on June 5. In 1995 he was honored at the 67th Academy Awards with the Jean Hersholt Award for humanitarian service. Quincy Jones was also named to President Clinton's Committee on the Arts and

Humanities. In 1996 he received the MusiCares Award for philanthropic giving from the National Academy of Recording Arts and Sciences. In 1997 he won the NAACP Image Award for Best Jazz Artist for *Q Live in Paris*.

While Quincy Jones certainly has a wide range of talents, perhaps his greatest contribution is his ability to cultivate the talents of other musicians while also expressing himself. "One of the most familiar names in music production—if not the entire entertainment industry—is Quincy Jones,"

Quincy's brothers Lloyd (right) and Richard (left) share the stage with Quincy as he receives an award. After Lloyd's death, Quincy included a moving tribute to his brother in the notes of his 1999 album From Q with Love.

announces the book *Creative Fire: African American Voices of Triumph*; Quincy is pictured surrounded by stars whose careers he helped make successful. Quincy says that the key to working with a performer is "remembering this person is a human being, and the human being has gifts. Love and respect force you to pay attention to all the intricacies of those gifts."

The Music Makers, an encyclopedia of musical figures, lists Quincy Jones as "an American composer and band leader." However, the entry on Quincy switches from trumpet playing to arranging the music of others. His vice presidency of Mercury Records, production of films and television shows like *Cannon*, and work as chief executive of Qwest make Q, as he is known to his friends, as much an arts administrator as a musician. Quincy Jones reinvented himself repeatedly over the years, moving from one adjacent career to the next—all of which used his creative, diverse, interpersonal skills. Quincy is at home in a wide range of musical styles from classical to popular; he is too big a man to be limited by any one genre, field of study, or line of work.

For too many years, the American dream of "liberty for all" was withheld from large sections of the U.S. population, most particularly blacks, women, and various ethnic and religious minorities. However, the dream of freedom was so strong that soon the vision of equality was extended to more of America's disenfranchised. Quincy Jones came to maturity at a unique time in American history when a war against fascism, the subsequent civil rights movement, a growing economy, technological development in electronics, and a new historical consciousness combined to allow a genius like Quincy to excel in a land that was slowly giving up discrimination as a way of life. A haven for immigrants—those who arrived voluntarily as well as slaves brought to these shores by force—America reaped the rewards of accepting talent from every color and creed. During Jones's lifetime, blacks began to take their

place on television—a medium invented when Quincy was young—as well as radio, film, and the boardrooms of arts and industry.

In Jones's personal life, he was able to overcome childhood poverty, the absence of a mother within a broken and reconstituted home, racial prejudice, and a near-fatal illness. While these hardships left scars—most notably in

An armful of 1991 Grammy Awards reflects the high esteem Quincy has won in the entertainment industry, which has continuously recognized and rewarded his unique and varied talents.

Quincy takes a break from a concert rehearsal with Tony Bennett (left) and Phil Collins. Now, nearing 70 years of age, this gifted artist, whose contributions to American music have spanned decades, has no intention of slowing down or retiring from the profession he loves.

a series of divorces and failed relationships—this gifted artist made an enormous contribution to the musical tradition he loved. In collaboration with others, he compensated for the family alliances he often failed to honor. Although Quincy was frequently absent in the lives of his own children, he served as a mentor and parental role model for other African-American brothers and sisters coming up in the music industry. Michael Jackson, for example, said of Quincy: "He was so father-like and so helpful. We built a camaraderie that was like a father-son type of friendship; he was always to the rescue and very loving. He has a very father-like charm. That's the main thing that's unique to him."

Looking ahead, Quincy Jones is not interested in slowing down. "I've seen what happens to guys when they retire. They just dry up. But I feel like I'm just starting out. I really do."

CHRONOLOGY

1933 Quincy Delight Jones Jr. born on March 14, in Chicago, Illinois, to Sarah Wells Jones and Quincy Delight Jones Sr.

1943 Quincy Sr. remarries; on July 4 the family moves to Bremerton, Washington

1945 Works at odd jobs as a paperboy, shoe-shine boy, strawberry picker, window washer, employee at a dry cleaners, and pinsetter at a bowling alley; sings in a gospel quartet

1947 Begins to study trumpet and makes first professional appearance on French horn jamming with a band at Bremerton YMCA

1948 Writes a suite called "From the Four Winds"; meets Ray Charles, Count Basie, Billie Holiday; joins Bumps Blackwell's band

1950 Takes music lessons from Clark Terry; wins musical scholarship to the University of Seattle

1951 Wins scholarship to Schillinger House of Music (now Berklee College of Music); moves to Boston, and later to New York, with girlfriend Jeri Caldwell; composition "Nocturne in Blue" is performed at a high school recital

1952 Quits school to join jazz performer Lionel Hampton on a tour of the South; arranges music for Oscar Pettiford

1953 Leaves New York for Oslo with Hampton on September 2; in Europe, plays jazz for sophisticated crowds; arranges music for Art Farmer, Clifford Brown, Gigi Gryce, Ray Anthony, Tommy Dorsey, James Moody, and Count Basie, and serves as a pianist during a recording session with Annie Ross in Stockholm; Jeri Caldwell gives birth to their daughter, Jolie Jones

1954 Arranges music for George Wallington

1955 Lives in New York and works with Benny Carter, Dinah Washington, Johnny Mathis, gospel pioneer James Cleveland, Clark Terry, and sax player Cannonball Adderley

1956 Arranges music for Paul Quinichette and Gene Krupa; plays trumpet and serves as music director for Dizzy Gillespie's band during State Department tour of Middle East and South America; begins recording for ABC-Paramount

1957 Takes job with Barclay Disque (the French distributor for Mercury Records) as head of musical operations in Paris; studies with Nadia Boulanger, the legendary Parisian tutor to American expatriate composers like Leonard Bernstein and Aaron Copeland

1958 Quincy wins awards for conducting and arranging in Sweden, Germany, and France

1959   Returns to New York and then tours Europe as music director for Harold Arlen's blues opera *Free and Easy*

1960   Tours Europe and the United States with Harold Arlen's band, which includes musicians Benny Bailey, Melba Liston, Phil Woods, Shihab, Jerome Richardson, and Budd Johnson; arranges music for an album by Ray Charles

1961   Hired by Mercury Records as a talent developer and head of the artists and repertory department after returning to the United States deep in debt

1962   Becomes the first black vice president in the music business with promotion by Mercury; wins first Grammy Award for scoring Ray Charles's "I Can't Stop Loving You" for Count Basie

1963   Works for Mercury Records in Holland, Italy, Great Britain, and Japan; records *Swinging at the Sands* with Frank Sinatra and various singles with Leslie Gore

1965   Leaves Mercury Records and moves to Hollywood, California, to work in the movie business; hired by Universal Pictures to score the movie *Mirage* with Gregory Peck; scores first feature film, *The Pawnbroker*, directed by Sidney Lumet

1966   Provides music for the ABC-TV series *Hey, Landlord*; Daughter Tina born; Jeri Jones and Quincy divorce

1967   First credited as music director for a television special, *Rodgers and Hart Today* (ABC); makes TV-movie debut with the score for *Ironside* (NBC)

1968   Son Quincy Delight Jones III born to Ulla Anderson and Quincy Jones

1969   Upon landing on the moon, astronaut Buzz Aldrin plays Quincy's arrangement of "Fly Me to the Moon" by Frank Sinatra; signs with A&M Records and releases album *Walking in Space*

1971   Receives Grammy for the album *Smackwater Jack*

1972   Becomes music director of *The New Bill Cosby Show*

1973   Receives Grammy for Best Instrumental Arrangement for "Summer in the City"

1974   Releases the best-selling album *Body Heat*; begins dating actress Peggy Lipton; in August, undergoes surgery for burst aneurysm; receives Gold Record for selling 500,000 copies of *Body Heat*; undergoes second brain surgery in October; divorces Ulla Anderson and marries Peggy Lipton in ceremony at her parents' Los Angeles home; daughter Kidada born

1975 Produces the Brothers Johnson's first album, *Look Out for Number 1,* and receives first Platinum Record for sales over a million copies

1976 "I Heard That" released; daughter Rashida born

1977 Scores Alex Haley's ABC-TV six-part miniseries *Roots* using ancient African rhythms

1978 Adapts music, provides songs, and serves as music supervisor for *The Wiz,* directed by Sidney Lumet

1979 Becomes Michael Jackson's producer for *Off the Wall*, which sells over eight million copies

1980 Founds his own label, Qwest Records

1981 Album *The Dude* receives an unprecedented twelve Grammy nominations and wins five Grammy Awards

1982 Makes feature debut as a song performer on the soundtrack of *The Last American Virgin*

1983 Receives eight Grammy nominations—the most ever received by a person in one year

1984 Helps raise money for Jesse Jackson's Presidential campaign; wins Grammy Award for Producer of the Year for *Thriller,* the album made with Michael Jackson which sold 40 million copies

1985 Produces "We Are the World," the best-selling single of all time, with 40 of the top recording artists; wins ABAA Music Award for efforts to aid African famine victims; coproduces film adaptation of Alice Walker's *The Color Purple*, which wins 11 Oscar nominations

1986 Marriage to Peggy Lipton collapses; goes to a South Pacific island to ward off a mental breakdown; provides theme song for *Oprah Winfrey Show*

1987 Returns to Los Angeles and produces Michael Jackson's album *Bad.* Qwest wins a Gold Album for *Substance*

1988 Begins work on multialbum project tracing history of African-American music from rock's roots in West Africa to rap. The record, released the next year, is called *Back on the Block*

1990 Wins Album of the Year at Grammy Awards for *Back on the Block*; receives French *Legion d'Honneur*; biographical film *Listen Up: The Lives of Quincy Jones* released; Peggy Lipton-Jones and Quincy divorce

1991 Becomes coproducer of Montreux Jazz and World Music Festival; helps launch NBC-TV's hit series *The Fresh Prince of Bel Air*, for which he acts as executive producer. Soundtrack album for *Boys N the Hood* released

1992 Establishes *VIBE* magazine

1993 Releases *Miles and Quincy Live at Montreux;* merges companies with David Salzman to form QDE, a co-venture with Time Warner, Inc. Quincy is co-CEO and chairman; actress Nastassja Kinski gives birth to Quincy's daughter, Kenya Julia Miambi Sara

1994 Receives Polar Music Prize in Stockholm, Sweden, and donates cash award of $128,000 to African National Congress; is named to President Bill Clinton's Committee on the Arts and Humanities; narrates documentary *A Great Day in Harlem*

1995 Releases from his QDE company a CD-ROM history of music: *479 A.D. to Today*; honored at 67th Academy Awards with Jean Hersholt Award for humanitarian service; puts out album *Q's Jook Joint*; becomes executive producer of the late-night variety show *Mad TV*

1996 Produces 68th Academy Awards show and telecast; receives MusiCares Award for philanthropic giving from National Academy of Recording Arts and Sciences

1997 Becomes executive producer of syndicated talk show *Vibe*; receives NAACP Image Award as Best Jazz Artist for *Q Live in Paris*

1998 Publishes *Blaze*, a magazine devoted to hip-hop music and culture; brother Lloyd Jones dies

1999 Mother Sarah Wells Jones dies of a stroke at age 94 in Seattle, Washington, on January 22; *From Q with Love* released

2000 Produced America's Millennium Gala, a musical concert and fireworks display held to usher in the millennium December 31, 1999–January 1, 2000

FURTHER READING

Andrews, Edmund L. "Listen Up! Quincy Jones Has a New Gig," *New York Times*, June 5, 1995.

Beers, Carole. "Sara Jones, Strong-Spirited Mother of Quincy Jones," *Seattle Times*, January 29, 1999.

Clayton, Janet. "Quincy Jones: Transforming America's Music into the World's," *Los Angeles Times,* March 31, 1995.

Dougherty, Steve. "Quincy Jones: He Has Hit High Notes in Every Genre from Bebop to Hip Hop; Now He's a Show Business Power," *People Magazine,* October 15, 1990.

Gates, Henry Louis. "Interview with Quincy Jones," PBS and WGBH/Frontline, 1998.

Gillen, Marilyn A. *Billboard Magazine*. May 20, 1995.

Graham, Nancy Perry. "Insider," *People Magazine*, March 8, 1999.

Gundersen, Edna. "Quincy Jones Packs 'Joint' with Talent," *USA Today*, November 7, 1995.

Haley, Alex. "Quincy Jones: A Candid Conversation with Pop's Master Builder about Rock, Rap, Racism, and His Thriller of a Career," July 1990, *The Playboy Interviews*. New York: Ballantine Books, 1993.

Holden, Stephen. "Pop View: A Pop Virtuoso Who Can Do It All," *New York Times*, December 3, 1989.

Horricks, Raymond. *Quincy Jones*. New York: Hippocrene Books, 1985.

Jones, Quincy. "Fifty Years of Black Music," *Ebony*, November, 1995.

Jones, Quincy. "Foreword" to *Snaps* by James Percelay, Monteria Ivey, and Stephen Dweck. New York: William Morrow and Company, 1994.

Jones, Quincy. Introduction to *The Encyclopedia of Jazz in the Seventies*, by Leonard Feather and Ira Gitler. New York: Horizon Press, 1976.

"Jones and Kinski Parents of Baby Girl," *Jet*, March 1, 1993.

Kallen, Stuart A. *Quincy Jones: I Have a Dream*. Edina, Minn: Abdo and Daughters, 1996.

Kernfeld, Barry, ed. *The New Grove Dictionary of Jazz*. Vol. I. Indianapolis: Macmillan Press, 1986.

Larkin, Colin, ed. *The Guinness Encyclopedia of Popular Music*. Vol. 2. Santa Rosa, Calif: Square One Books, 1992.

Lynn Farnol Group, Inc., eds. *American Society of Composers, Authors, and Publishers Biographical Dictionary*, New York: ASCAP, 1966.

Matney, William, ed. *Who's Who Among Black Americans*. Lake Forest, Ill: Educational Communications, 1988.

Morse, Steve. "A 26-Song Valentine from Quincy Jones," *Boston Globe*, February 7, 1999.

Newman, Bruce. "A Cosmic Q Rating," *Los Angeles Times*, November 5, 1995.

Ross, Courtney Sale, ed. *Listen Up: The Lives of Quincy Jones*. New York: Warner Books, 1990.

Shah, Diane K. "On Q," *New York Times*, November 18. 1990.

Strauss, Neil. "The Pop Life." *Creative Fire*. Alexandria, Va: Time-Life Books, 1994.

Unger-Hamilton, Clive, ed. *The Music Makers*. New York: Harry N. Abrams, 1979.

INDEX

PICTURE CREDITS

Linda Bayer has an M.A. in psychology and studied for an Ed.D. at the Graduate School of Education at Harvard University. She also has an M.A. in English and a Ph.D. in humanities. Dr. Bayer has worked with patients suffering from substance abuse and other problems at Judge Baker Guidance Center and within the Boston public school system. She served on the faculties of several universities, including Boston University and the Hebrew University in Israel, where she occupied the Sam and Ayala Zacks Chair and was twice a writer in residence in Jerusalem.

Dr. Bayer was a newspaper editor and syndicated columnist, winning the Simon Rockower Award for excellence in journalism. She is the author of hundreds of articles and is working on her 15th book. She has written for a number of public figures, including General Colin Powell and President Bill Clinton. She is currently a senior writer and strategic analyst at the White House.

Dr. Bayer is the mother of two children, Lev and Ilana.

James Scott Brady serves on the board of trustees with the Center to Prevent Handgun Violence and is the vice chairman of the Brain Injury Foundation. Mr. Brady served as assistant to the President and White House press secretary under President Ronald Reagan. He was severely injured in an assassination attempt on the president, but remained the White House press secretary until the end of the administration. Since leaving the White House, Mr. Brady has lobbied for stronger gun laws. In November 1993, President Bill Clinton signed the Brady Bill, a national law requiring a waiting period on handgun purchases and a background check on buyers.